Advance Praise for

American Newspeak

American Newspeak is just what we need in these
mad days: a funny guide to the serious assaults on
our language, our culture, our minds.

— Howard Zinn

Freshly baked humor direct from the website
rated "the best" on the web in political satire
by Yahoo's Internet Life

American Newspeak slices and dices the lies
of our culture. It's the funniest book I've read
since The Enron Code of Ethics.

— Paul Loeb, author of *Soul of a Citizen*

In a world where armies don't retreat, but make
"tactical advances to the rear" and your grocer
needs your social security number "to better serve
you," *American Newspeak* cuts through all the
doubletalk in a sharp, humorous way.

— George Rabe in the HotBot Directory

Considering the absurdity of what is (and is not) covered by the news media, *American Newspeak* is a natural reaction to the banality that typifies what passes for news nowadays. *Newspeak* blends a caustic wit with a terse style to deconstruct the news stories of the day...

— Paul Fleming in Web Active

American Newspeak collects morsels of news pieces and exposes their double meanings, offering an often satiric commentary on politics and culture.

— Excite website Guide

American Newspeak presents cerebral, humorous commentary on current events. It's a thoughtful digestion of news, followed by withering, caustic comments... Jay Leno it's not, but a sort of mild Dennis Miller it is.

— *Internet Directory for Dummies*

AMERICAN NEWSPEAK

AMERICAN NEWSPEAK

THE MANGLING OF MEANING FOR POWER AND PROFIT

Wayne Grytting

NEW SOCIETY PUBLISHERS

Cataloguing in Publication Data:

A catalog record for this publication is available from the National Library of Canada.

Copyright © 2002 by Wayne Grytting.
All rights reserved.

Cover design by Diane McIntosh. Cover image: US National Archives.

Printed in Canada by Transcontinental Printing.

Paperback ISBN: 0-86571-464-9

Inquiries regarding requests to reprint all or part of *American Newspeak: The Mangling of Meaning for Power and Profit* should be addressed to New Society Publishers at the address below.

To order directly from the publishers, please add $4.50 shipping to the price of the first copy, and $1.00 for each additional copy (plus GST in Canada). Send check or money order to:

New Society Publishers
P.O. Box 189, Gabriola Island, BC V0R 1X0, Canada
1-800-567-6772

New Society Publishers' mission is to publish books that contribute in fundamental ways to building an ecologically sustainable and just society, and to do so with the least possible impact on the environment, in a manner that models this vision. We are committed to doing this not just through education, but through action. We are acting on our commitment to the world's remaining ancient forests by phasing out our paper supply from ancient forests worldwide. This book is one step towards ending global deforestation and climate change. It is printed on acid-free paper that is **100% old growth forest-free (100% post-consumer recycled),** processed chlorine free, and printed with vegetable based, low VOC inks. For further information, or to browse our full list of books and purchase securely, visit our website at: www.newsociety.com

NEW SOCIETY PUBLISHERS   www.newsociety.com

Dedicated to

the CEO's, advertisers, PR experts,
journalists and politicians whose unbridled manipulation
of the once proud English language has made this book possible.
Thanks folks, for helping a poor, dull individual enter the exciting
field of humor writing just by quoting your words.
May you make your way through the fog.

Contents

Acknowledgments

As a writer, I'm a somewhat awkward toddler who's been supported for years by the efforts of others. Those who know the Scandinavian family I sprouted from will easily recognize the sources of my satirical voice. I can just hear one of my aunts saying, "He sounds just like Arnold." My father was a commercial halibut fisherman who taught the fine art of the practical joke and the not-too-subtle comeback. And if my writing has heart, I owe much of that to my mother, Esther Grytting, who's been quietly caring for others and holding heads above water for over eighty years. The less said about my brother Harold, the better, except for his brief encounter with sanity when he married Cathy. Last, but least, I should mention a young woman named Karena, who makes wild claims about me being her father. We still have hopes the remedial humor classes will take hold with her. Thank you, Karena, not only for helping with the book but for becoming an all-round good person.

American Newspeak began as a weekly column on the Internet in 1996. My first distributor was Hank Roth and his Progressive News mailing list. To my surprise, Lydia Sargent and *Z Magazine* decided to pick up the column as a regular feature and actually paid money for my verbiage. This helped finance a two-day vacation to Tukwila, Washington. Much to my embarrassment, the ring-in-the-nose crowd also picked up on my Orwellian reporting, and I found my column appearing in *Eat the State*, edited by Geov Parrish and Maria Tomchick. Then the *Progressive Populist* and a swarm of freeloading Web sites jumped on the bandwagon. Next was the radio: Seattle KCMU radio producer Mike McCormick took me under his wing to do commentary. My greatest honor was being picked up by a public radio station in northern Saskatchewan. Thanks, gang. In the meantime, a community of "informers" began e-mailing in examples of cutting-edge advances in Newspeak. Most of those names I've managed to lose. My humble apologies. Here are a few of the contributors whose names I was able to retrieve, who've made this book possible: Jake Sexton, Doug Honig, Carrie McClaren, Phil Kos, Andy Cahn, Mark Glyde, Cynthia Bock-Goodener, Kurt Cockrum, David West, William Leler, Marie Birnbaum, Tom Langdon, Adam Connelly, Dante Tanenbaum, Ann Ramage, Sam Windholz, Burke Day, and Dave Steele.

As I slowly accumulated piles of contemporary Newspeak, it dawned on me that I could cut and paste it into a book. This step required a bit of work, but a manuscript was born. I then had the job of twisting the arms of friends to read and critique it. Here is a list of people I owe thanks to, whether I feel like giving it or not. Thanks to my old Reed housemate Eric Manzer for insisting I improve my comic rhythm and for pushing me up Mt. Rainier. To Gary Moresky for insightful commentary and for that one second atop Silver Peak when I had him convinced we'd climbed the wrong mountain. To my longtime friend Paul Loeb for all the mistakes he made ahead of me and was so willing to share — keep making them. To Rebecca Hughes for doing an excellent editing job and for so kindly putting up with Paul. To Sarah Patton, whom I first met as a high school debater, for so many excellent news tips. To Jane Hatfield, my favorite "ex," for her great proofreading and encouragement (and to Mary, too). To my Southern correspondent and old friend Maarten Ultee for passing along so many Newspeak stories from Alabama. To Patrice Conway for that wonderful line, "I wanted to be a follower, but the leaders were all lost." To the fine legal mind of Barbara Wilkins that tore apart an early version of the last chapter. To the steady stream of humor and support I've had from Verna Harms and Steve Lewis. The list goes on.

Going a bit further afield, I want to extend thanks to the many crewmembers I've fished with in Alaska on boats like the *Guardian*, the *Viking Spirit*, the *Mark Christopher*, and the *Bergen*, who helped sharpen my meager wits — with the exception of Pete Knudsen. To my old coffee house discussion partners like Norm Fischer, Rick Angell, Murray Cooper, Alan Walworth (Where are you, Alan?), Joe Peschek, Marilyn Chase, and Jack Schillinger. All have helped deepen my understanding. To my Zen Abbot Genjo Marinelli for sitting so patiently beside an open door. To the members of the Dai Bai Zai sangha for tolerating not only my giggling fits during meditation but all kinds of other assorted behavioral quirks. To the students and staff at Washington Middle School for providing daily inspiration for a budding humorist. We all need to thank the fine people at New Society, who were stuck with the unenviable job of publishing this book. Thanks, Chris, Michael, and the rest of the troops up there in British Columbia.

Finally, I want to thank a very special woman, who became my wife a year ago. After 20 years as one of the first female longshore workers on the docks of Seattle, Kevin Castle decided she was ready for the challenge of handling more volatile cargo. I've loved every minute of it. Thank you, Kevin, for the powerhouse of a person you are, for the wisdom you've earned, for the family and community you brought with you, and for the love and joy you share with me each day.

Introduction

AFTER THE TRAGEDY of September 11th, a tiny window opened in America's cultural landscape. Besides feeling vulnerable and outraged, many people paused to engage in an activity quite foreign to our customs, an activity that required journeying into the most infrequently visited regions of the cerebral cortex, an activity known as — reflection. And what we reflected about were the complaints that flooded in from around the world that Americans are shallow, self-centered, and materialistic.

Let's be open about this. We are. And we're doing a damn good job of selling it to the rest of the world. So there. But critics of America's superficiality leave unanswered a lot of really nifty questions, like, just how shallow is America? How shallow can you get if you really try? Can you make advances in narcissism? Can spiritual aspirations be met with a new toaster oven? Can a society be united by shared memories of advertising jingles? How long can a TV news anchor smile? How much of yourself can you sell and still have brain cells left to tie your shoes? These are the issues you are about to see cracked wide open as we explore the cutting-edge advances being made in one of our nation's leading industries: Newspeak.

1

Newspeak and Doublethink were the brain children of George Orwell's *1984*. Orwell may have missed the boat with his prediction of a totalitarian leader with a moustache ruling every aspect of our lives, but he hit the mark with his picture of how our language could be dumbed down and the mind turned into a bureaucratic morass. Newspeak, for Orwell, was language after it had been run over by semi-trucks, leaving the road littered with nicely flattened out concepts like "downsizing," "networking," "interfacing," and those nice, friendly monosyllables we get to hear strung together on TV newscasts. Doublethink, or Doublespeak, refers to the delightful contradictions those smashed words could be twisted into by practitioners who just didn't let their minds in on the fact. This mental gridlock produces scenes like former President Bill Clinton condemning campaign contributions on his way to a fundraising dinner in Chicago. Or President George W. Bush telling school children, "One way to fight evil is to fight it with kindness and love and compassion" — on the 36th day of our bombing of Afghanistan.

The fact that our "best and brightest" politicians and corporate PR types are regularly spouting Doublespeak is not exactly a new discovery (as my dear mother was kind enough to inform me). What your average crusty cynic fails to appreciate is the pace of innovation in the field. Newspeak does not stand still. It's dynamic. Each year it's new and improved. Every month countless individuals are not only making advances, but cutting-edge advances. America has been leaving Orwell's *1984* in the dust. Without the benefit of a Big Brother, America's practitioners have been showing what teamwork can do, raising Orwell's standards of Doublethink to new heights, making it rightly one of our most important export products. And receiving so little recognition for their efforts ...

The scope of the advances in the Newspeak industry hit me after I'd seen a particularly intriguing ad on television. It featured a woman at a grocery check-out counter unloading products with very familiar names as a voice from on high explained: "A friend is someone you know about, someone you can trust. A brand's a bit like that. You meet this friend through advertising ... Without advertising, how would you recognize your friends?" This fine commercial was sponsored by the International Advertising Association and was part of a series of ads appearing in more than 200 countries. After watching it I was left with warm fuzzy feelings for all my friends — Nabisco, General Mills, Nestle. Yes, I love you, Big Brother.

"Without advertising, how would you recognize your friends?" Despite appearances, this question was not written by a total airhead. It represents probably one of the finer literary products of a highly educated mind, undoubtedly trained in some of our nation's elite schools before advancing to Madison Avenue, a person exposed to a minimum of 17 years of public or private school tutoring (for a possible total of 19,440 hours of education). Assuming the ad text was not written by a committee (how could it?), it had to pass muster with a minimum of, let's say, a dozen ad executives representing a possible grand total of 233,280 hours of instruction by some of our nation's leading educators. This, I suggest, is the real crisis of our education system.

Nature abhors a vacuum, and the absence of Hitler-style dictators and herds of official Thought Police has brought forth worthy replacements. This became clear to me one day at a Barnes & Noble bookstore in an upscale shopping mall in Seattle. I had barely settled into browsing through the remainders rack when a voice came on the public address system announcing that He would be appearing in only 15 minutes. I'm sure you've guessed it already. If you haven't you will need to read further. Yes, none other than Ronald McDonald was coming to make a guest appearance at the store.

I quickly looked around at my fellow customers. No one was gagging, no one even blinked or shook their head in disbelief. They simply went about grazing through the shelves. But there I was, having a religious experience right in the middle of the remainders rack, a virtual epiphany (I think that's what the word is). Ronald McDonald at such a fine upstanding bookstore, as if to finally welcome the literary world into the realm of hamburgers and soft drinks. It was like everything had come full circle. McDonald's, Walt Disney, Pepsi, Chevron, Chrysler, Wal-Mart, Denny's, the U.S. Senate — we were all one big happy corporate clan. We were all fellow commodities. Big Brother by committee. And now fully out of the closet.

It's hard for the uninitiated to appreciate how the classic advances of past eras could be improved upon. For example, in the 1940s, Americans who'd fought earlier against fascism in Spain, when our nation remained neutral, were labeled "premature anti-fascists" by the Defense Department. How do you improve on that? Or consider the many examples from the "golden age," the 1980s, as chronicled by William Lutz in his two fine books on Doublespeak. Who can forget George Bush Sr.'s replacement of the well-known concept of "new taxes" with "revenue enhancement," or the Pentagon's description of the 1983 invasion of Grenada as a "predawn vertical insertion" or their replacement of the phrase "neutron bomb" with "radiation enhancement device" or their elevation of the lowly shovel to a "combat emplacement evacuator" or their seminal discovery of the term "collateral damage" for civilian deaths?

The private sector was hard-pressed to keep pace with such advances but try they did, with top honors going to corporations dealing with the difficult problem of saying goodbye to trusted employees. Although "downsizing," a model of proper Newspeak, beat all comers for its elegant simplicity, other contenders demonstrated the creative dynamic powering the dumbing-down of discourse. For example, who can forget Bell Labs' use of "involuntary separation from payroll" in place of the older phrase "your ass has been canned"? Or Wal-Mart's kindness in merely subjecting employees to a "normal payroll adjustment"? Better yet was GM's "career transition program." And in the all-important Miss Manners appropriate speech division, let us not forget the efforts of the hospital industry to replace death with "negative patient care outcome."

Worthy as these classic examples are, it is my firm conviction that contemporary Newspeak, or what I like to call "postmodern

Newspeak," presents a vastly expanded terrain for the mangling of meaning. The postmodern era in thickheadedness began officially with the ending of the Cold War, an event that allowed the passing of the baton from the Pentagon to Corporate America. For the first time since the days of the Roaring Twenties, corporate executives came fully out of the closet. Without the menace of International Communism or even hippie sons and daughters raising eyebrows, the rich stormed out from behind country club walls like herds of ravenous wolves. If Newspeak hounds like I. F. Stone could once best hunt their prey by following the trails of politicians' speeches through the pages of the Congressional Record, in the postmodern era the "action" had shifted to the pages of *The Wall Street Journal* and *Advertising Age* as executives openly bared their souls right in front of the servants while politicians ran errands for them. Elite conversations about how best to manage public perceptions, manipulate employees, commercialize every nook and cranny of daily life, flaunt status and wealth — all came right out in the open, screaming, "Free at last! Free at last!"

Seeing the obvious need for public recognition for so many pioneering efforts in language and logic, I began rummaging through the back pages of some of our nation's finer newspapers and posting reports on the Internet at my low-tech American Newspeak website (www.americannewspeak.org). Before I knew it, other people were swamping me with their own examples. Finally I had a use for the one skill that too many years of commercial fishing in Alaska had taught me — knowing when to put on my hip boots. The result is this collection of Greatest Hits from the Web site, a Whitman's Chocolate Sampler of the varieties of shallowness in a full-blown consumer society, blatantly modeled on the Audubon Society's *Field Guide to North American Birds*.

To gain the proper aesthetic appreciation for the advances made from Orwell's time, you need to know some of the basic tools used by connoisseurs to separate the wheat from the chaff (students should get out your yellow markers). For those of you who slept through their high school Senior Lit class, Orwell's *1984* is about a middle-aged man named Winston Smith who's having a mid-life crisis (I guarantee you some graduate student somewhere has seriously argued this thesis). Surrounded by two-way television sets monitoring his every move and patriotic zealots ready to report any sign of disloyalty, he is, inconvenienced a bit in some substandard accommodations, caught by the omnipresent Thought Police, which leads him to rat on his girlfriend and to rediscover his love for Big Brother. By book's end he's fully prepared to agree that 2 + 2 = 5 or to write copy for Madison Avenue about how brand names are our friends. Beyond that, the novel presents a model of what Orwell believed was happening to our language and logic as it became corrupted by centralized powers, a world where the language of Newspeak "made all other modes of thought impossible."

To grasp how quality Newspeak works, we must import our one Official Concept (the only one I could afford) which I call "wallage." The term "wallage" refers to the building of defensive fortifications that cut us off from ourselves and others and birds and warbling brooks etc. It can be used in phrases like "The boss has a lot of wallage today" or "Texaco experienced a wallage deficit" (i.e., someone blabbed the truth). I'm told that men, for example, often display high wallage in relationships, but I have no evidence to support this claim. Newspeak, in this usage, is any high wallage language used as a means of control by a powerful elite. And cutting-edge advances in this field? This would refer to architectural achievements in building even higher walls to shut out distasteful realities.

Once your defenses are in place you are ready for the next step: pigeonholing. Orwell's Newspeak was built upon reducing language to a simple set of monosyllables — simple fixed slots to put units of experience into. More complex thoughts were then made by smashing together pigeonholes to give us wonderful concepts like "goodthink (orthodoxy), "goodsex" (chastity), and "doubleplusgood" (wonderful). Adjectives and adverbs took a real beating while verbs were reduced to a few simple forms. Words deemed inappropriate for the masses were simply "disappeared" by the Thought Police, much like any idea more complex than a soundbite is cut out by our TV news. As one of the scribes of the Newspeak dictionary explained in *1984*, "In the end, we shall make Thoughtcrime literally impossible, because there shall be no words in which to express it."

Mowing down the wild undergrowth of metaphors and traditional expressions and replacing it with a putting green of uniform word units make possible mankind's greatest step since electric hairdryers — i.e., the automation of thought. (Individual thought always was so redundant). The efficiencies offered by this step can be seen in an example I've picked at random, so common everyone will guess the ending. In 1999, a Guatemalan woman applied for asylum in the U.S. after fleeing a husband who had repeatedly raped, kicked, and pistol-whipped her. Government attorneys not only openly admitted these facts but also admitted she faced more harm if she returned home. An old-fashioned judge might have thought hard about this case and rendered a difficult decision. Very inefficient. This is a no-brainer for today's Immigration and Naturalization Service. It was as if she had entered a McDonald's and tried to order spaghetti. Not on the menu. The INS had five meals on its menu for human rights appeals (race, religion, nationality, political opinion, and social group), and she didn't fit any. Asylum denied. Case closed. No thought required. Just the simple automation we can see every day in the workings of any fast-food restaurant.

As we increase our distance from the world, we end up building larger and more efficient Newspeak factories. School administrations reduce learning to numerical percentiles, corporations reduce complex environmental questions to quarterly profits, advertisers reduce every personal problem to consumption. We're left with a flattened out reality, a linguistic parking lot, a conceptual sheep ranch. These too are "advances." Just as we have progress in scientific knowledge, so we also have advances in obtuseness. Just as higher organisms evolve, so do the lower ones ...

Although most connoisseurs of Orwellian speech delight in finding evidences of Newspeak in the crevices of organizations, I must say my tastes run toward finding quality Doublethink. For

Orwell, Doublethink stood at the Newspeak summit. This term is conferred on statements displaying the workings of a mind able to hold contradictory thoughts without the slightest hint of a problem. It becomes possible when the brain "evolves" to the point where it can't translate memos from one side to another. It's Dan Rather denouncing the media circus around the O.J. Simpson trial without his brain registering the minor fact that he was a circus ringleader. Or State Department officials denouncing terrorists while we rain bombs on Iraq and Afghanistan. Or narcissistic yuppies denouncing ... narcissistic yuppies. Or the quagmires of military logic immortalized by Joseph Heller in his novel *Catch-22*. His war-razzled characters confronted regulations that allowed only insanity as grounds for getting out of combat duty, with the "minor" amendment that "anyone who wants to get out of combat duty really isn't crazy" and so could not avoid duty. Checkmate. No exit.

Finally let me issue a few disclaimers. Now that I've primed you on the theme of Newspeak, I should confess I'm not very good at staying within the lines, and some of these news reports do wander off-trail occasionally. It's also been brought to my attention that some of my remarks appear to belong to a genre known as satire. This can be dangerous. Several years ago a trendy Microsoft online magazine named *Slate* advertised in magazines with these words: "It's what everyone is talking about, media, politics, technology, high and low culture ... all with a certain insouciant smirk that thinking people find compelling." Let me say what a disappointment it was to flunk their "thinking people" test. I'm hoping to recover soon. I should also confess I secretly ran to a dictionary to discover the term "insouciant" means "blithely indifferent."

This book is not about running around sporting "insouciant smirks," even though that sounds like great fun. We are not offering defensive fig leaves for "thinking people" to hide behind while sipping their lattes. This book is about some very real dead canaries in our civic life. But more importantly, it is about what we must do to penetrate the walls that render our shallow cultural air unbreathable. How do we communicate with administrators, academics, and corporate executives busy manipulating us like a lower species? How do we resuscitate people whose lives have been reduced to a circuit between jobs, shopping malls, and TV sets? How do we challenge the daily barrage of advertising conditioning us to consume, consume, and then (did I mention) consume? How can we reclaim community landscapes overrun by corporate and bureaucratic dinosaurs? I have attempted to address a few of these issues in the final chapter. If I remember correctly, it has something to do with using creativity, play, and humor to bridge the ramparts. I've also included, at no extra cost, Helpful Hints at the end of each chapter to encourage appropriate responses to excesses of "Newspeakian" zeal. Good luck.

The Depths of Shallowness

W HEN THE MAKERS OF TEEN TALK BARBIE had finally mastered the technology of cramming tape-recorded sentences into the foot-high doll, they were faced with the daunting challenge of deciding what the famous icon's first words would be. Mattel came up with the following: "I love shopping," "Meet me at the mall," and "Math is hard." This is as good as it gets in America.

Even among experts, there's a lot of debate over how to gauge advances in shallowness. The quality I give the most points for is general obliviousness. While many people repress the knowledge that we are turning the planet into a parking lot, more are just clueless. These are people who consider *Hollywood Tonight* deep. These are people who were genuinely surprised to learn that some people in the Third World dislike us (undoubtedly because of our "freedom"). They don't live in a world where people go hungry, but in a happy virtual reality bounded by MTV, *Baywatch*, and weekly trips to the cathedral — the shopping mall. These are our legacy to the world.

TOUrist Meccas

It's quiz time. Guess what our most popular spot for tourists is: the Liberty Bell, the Grand Canyon, Graceland, Walt Disney World, or the Alamo? All wrong. By far, the largest bio-mass of tourists has been going to discount shopping malls. The Travel Industry of America reported that shopping is far and away the most popular activity for travelers. In Philadelphia, for instance, the 215-store Franklin Mills Mall drew an estimated six million tourists, four times as many as the Liberty Bell. America's most popular mall was the 400-store Mall of America in Bloomington, Minnesota, which drew twelve million tourists, "more than Walt Disney World, the Grand Canyon and Graceland combined." *The Wall Street Journal* proudly declared, "Now, shopping is the vacation." Signaling this change was a Vermont travel brochure that promised "The Best Hiking in Vermont." In place of rugged mountain trails, it displayed a collection of shopping malls.

QUALITY TIME WITH Nature

American consumers are offered a way to get back to nature without ever having to leave the safety of their favorite shopping malls. The Ogden Corporation, taking advantage of their vast experience catering airplane food, opened eight American Wilderness exhibits as part of what they call "shoppertainment." For a mere $10, customers can view 60 different animal species in six different wilderness settings, traveling through desert, forest, mountain, valley, and seashore ecosystems. To enhance the experience, artificial trees and plants were added as well as hidden canisters that emitted natural fragrances. After a brief tour, customers are returned to their natural habitat, the mall, where they can shop at the Naturally Untamed Boutique or eat in the Wilderness Grill. The experience, says Ogden VP Jonathan Stern, is ideal for "people who prefer nature in small doses." (Isn't that the best way?) Stern adds that people are so accustomed to hurrying today, the average visit to the Grand Canyon is only 22 minutes long, coincidentally the same length as the average TV show minus commercials. Time for another channel, I guess.

aırHeaD ProTecTioN DePT.

The New Jersey Supreme Court ruled that shopping malls must allow access to citizens who want to engage in peaceful leafletting. Lost in the clamor for free speech was any concern for those who could be harmed by unbridled speech in our citadels of consumption. Raising this issue was Nancy Sterling, spokesperson for the Wells Park Group. She declared, "Our bottom line is customers deserve an intrusion-free shopping environment." Going even further was Mark Shoifet, spokesperson for the International Council of Shopping Centers, who warned the Court's ruling would "place an undue burden on the malls of New Jersey, their tenants and especially on their customers." This marked the first time in history the reading of leaflets and the prospect of having to think about the issues raised have been recognized for the "undue burden" they place on shoppers. Hopefully, activists will have felt duly chastised.

BarBie'S BaD DaY

Have you ever had one of those days when everything you do just seems to turn out wrong? Well, that's the kind of year Mattel Toys has been having with Barbie, the doll they say gives "the message to young girls that they can be anything they want to be." Mattel tried to counter Barbie's stodgy, white, middle-class image by introducing diversity into her world. They even allowed "diverse" workers in China to assemble Barbie and her friends for $1.20 a day. But that only led to people boycotting Barbie. So Mattel developed a wheelchair-bound friend for Barbie and everybody applauded. Christened "Share a Smile Becky," she was intended by Mattel to help change people's attitudes toward the handicapped. That should have kept the critics happy, but it did not. No, it seems there was a small glitch. Barbie's world, it was discovered, was not wheelchair accessible. Becky's wheelchair couldn't fit through the doors of Barbie's Dream House or her Malibu House, so Becky couldn't party with Ken. How true to life our toys are today.

THE TIGHTENING CIRCLE

One of the most telling details about American attitudes toward civic life transpired when Dial soap announced they were dumping their classic advertising slogan, "Aren't you glad you use Dial?" The jingle's demise, I suggest, may provide anthropologists of the future with major insights into postmodern culture. In the words of *The Wall Street Journal*, the slogan "wasn't relevant any longer because of what is going on inside of soap users' heads." (Don't laugh, at least they report something going on.) Dial's ad agency argued that people today are not primarily worried about offending others with body odor, but mainly want protection from the germs of the outside world. In the words of DDB Needham ad executive Joe Belmonte, "It used to be 'I'm trying to make myself presentable to you.' Now it's more about 'I've got to wash you off of me'."

In a similar vein was a report on a change in the way fences are built. It used to be that the "good side" of the planks faced one's neighbors and the framing was on the inside. This custom has now been reversed in most "better" neighborhoods. I guess you could call it "keeping up with the Jones' narcissism."

THOREAU ON WHEELS

Are you interested in "Backpacking Chevy Van Style," or do you even understand the concept? If not, you need to catch a trend-setting ad from Chevrolet's RV department. Since the literary style of the ad's text far exceeds my meager abilities to reproduce it, let me just quote it at length: "Years ago, you used to go backpacking to smell the flowers, watch the sunset and just get away from it all. A sleeping bag and a mess kit were all you needed. Well, now that you are used to life's luxuries, it takes more." Just imagine being out in nature without a TV and dishwasher? Or even a cell phone? And when you "backpack" Chevy Van style, you can, because of its powerful Vortec engine or optional 6.5 liter turbocharged diesel V8, "count on years of communing with nature in reliable ruggedness." For an even fuller "communion with nature," you might try revving the engine.

Similarly, Chrysler Daimler's Jeep Grand Cherokee has been, we are told in a magazine ad, "ingenuously engineered to help you escape the metropolis — just not its luxuries." Finally the solution to the age-old dilemma of not being able to have your cake and eat it too. Cynics might compare it to escaping prison in a portable prison cell, but let us ignore them for now. Besides the usual luxuries that cultured people like me have come to expect in a fine car (like a steering wheel, a brake pedal, and extra duct tape), the Jeep Grand Cherokee comes equipped with a mini-trip computer, radio stations for two, and a Homelink Universal Transmitter. This item controls not only your garage door and home security system but also, and I quote from the ad, your "estate gate." Estate gate?! It's a bleeping Jeep we're talking about. In an ad in a publication reaching some 800,000 readers, it's just naturally assumed everyone has a gate for their estate. Ah, but it gets better. It turns out all these accoutrements for "roughing it" are, say the ad writers, "more of a necessity than a luxury." I know just how true those words are. I remember how tough it was when my estate gate broke down. Damn neighbor's dog ... but enough of my trials and tribulations.

Designer Marxism

Romans would chain their conquered opponents and parade them through the Coliseum. We have different means. A new edition of *The Communist Manifesto* came out, described by Verso publisher Colin Robinson as "elegant enough to grace a coffee table." Marx and Engels have earned their place next to *Vogue* and *Gentleman's Quarterly* because of the trend towards "revolutionary chic." Thanks also to its red-tinged pages and stylish red ribbon, both Borders and Barnes & Noble featured the book. Meanwhile, Barney's department store in New York reportedly featured the book, along with a selection of red lipsticks, in its windows as "conceptual art." Barney's creative director Simon Doonan said, "It's OK to look at the book as camp." In this light he suggests the book could, if given an attached handle, "make a snazzy accessory to a designer dress."

Meanwhile, Cuba's major revolutionary export, Che Guevera, was back in vogue with a best-selling memoir, and several biographies and movies came out about him. This was a result of the fact that, to quote *The New York Times*, "his image has become more vivid, complex and commercial." For example, Raichle Molitar, distributors of Fischer's Revolution Skis, held a Che look-a-like contest to sell their skis. Explained spokesperson Jim Fleischer, "We felt that the Che image — just the icon and not the man's doings — represented what we wanted: revolution, extreme change." This corporate pursuit of revolution, of just the icon and not the reality, is also helping to sell Swatch watches and even ashtrays. All of this commercialization has left Cubans somewhat mystified, but then what can you expect from a country without a single McDonald's.

New Frontiers in Intimacy

Ken Behring, a California real estate tycoon and one-time owner of the Seattle Seahawks football team, pioneered an advance in the art of conducting extramarital affairs worthy of our postmodern age. Mr. Behring liked to have "companionship" on his long vacation treks away from his wife. To protect himself, he had his chief financial officer draw up a form for his traveling partners that is state of the art. It reads: "I recognize that conversation and conduct of a sexual nature may take place on this trip. I have voluntarily accepted Ken's invitation. I agree that I will not bring any suit or make any financial or other claim of any kind against Ken that is in any way related to the trip." Do note the fine blend of legal and personal language in this passage. This advance is offset on the other side by a growing trend among newlyweds reported by Reuters — the renting of wedding rings "in case things don't work out."

Bible Improvements

In the 1990s, Bible sales went into a slump. As a result, Bible publishers went out and surveyed their customers only to discover numerous complaints that The Book was too difficult to read. The result, reported *The New York Times*, was an "industry trend to simplified text." The Tyndale House, for example, put 90 scholars to work for seven years to produce a "modernized" translation. And what does "modernized" mean? It turns out to be a text pitched at a sixth-grade reading level. Or, to quote the book jacket I cleverly tracked down in a Seattle bookstore, the new translation has resulted in a "wonderful balance of readability and authority," thus making the Bible "accessible, useful and enjoyable for every situation." Sadly, they forgot the "new and improved" and "50% brighter" parts of the ad ... And not to be outdone, Harper Collins has upped the ante with its New International Version pitched at a mind-numbing third-grade reading level. I'm told it reads like the NBC Nightly News.

DEFENDING THE FATHERLAND

Faced with increased immigration of foreign speakers to our shores, 22 U.S. states have responded by declaring English our official language. Now a number of small towns have gone a step further and passed laws penalizing linguistic "infringements." In Norcross, Georgia, Maria Cobarrubias was fined $115 for the name sign posted outside the supermarket she owns saying "Supermercado Jalisco." She had violated Norcross' ordinance banning signs that are less than 75% English "as determined by local authorities." The law, which ostensibly was passed for safety reasons, has also been used against several Korean churches and an Oriental beauty shop. The good news: Norcross Sgt. H. Smith believes some Spanish words are "acceptable," which should be cause for massive celebrations in Norcross' Hispanic community.

The Allied Insurance Company struck a blow for the use of the English language when they fired two workers for speaking Spanish without authorization. Unfortunately, a little confusion was created by the fact that the two workers had been hired for their ability to speak Spanish. Or, more precisely, the two Spanish-speaking women had been hired, said co-owner Linda Polk, "to speak Spanish to non-American-speaking people" — but not to each other. Despite their outreach efforts to "non-American-speaking people," the company held firm to the principle that theirs was an English-speaking office. They even sent out an official memo about their policy, but to no avail. The two offenders refused to sign the memo because they didn't want their heritage taken away, or some such trivial reason, and had to be fired on the spot. The bottom line? Basic etiquette. Mrs. Polk said the two were "being very rude for speaking in a language we don't understand." And Miss Manners says always fire rude employees.

BUY AMERICAN

In 1997, six of the top eight finishers in Colorado's Bolder Boulder Marathon were from Kenya. But sharp-eyed corporate sponsors immediately spotted a problem with this result. The Kenyan runners were "marketing liabilities." So to ensure more Americans finished among the leaders, race officials passed a new rule limiting the number of runners from Kenya, or any other foreign country, to three. But it's the justification for this change, presented by race director Bill Reef, that earns particular merit. "We hope to level the playing field," said Mr. Reef in what is believed to be the first time American athletes have received protection from a nation with an average income worth less than two pairs of Nikes. Then Mr. Reed enunciated what could become the sports world's own Monroe Doctrine: "It's our country, our event, our money. American sponsors want American winners, or at least Americans among the top finishers." To "level the playing field" even more, sponsors have promised to double the prize money for our athletes who finish in the top five.

DUMBING DOWN DEPT.

A federal judge affirmed the inalienable right of American communities to refuse to hire people who are too intelligent. The town of New London, Connecticut, has for years been hiring new police officers on the basis of an intelligence test. Those who score too high, correctly answering more than 27 of the 50 questions (or more than 54%), are routinely flunked from consideration on the grounds they will become bored with the drudgery of chasing criminals and eating donuts. When an over-intelligent candidate named Robert Jordan challenged this policy in court, U.S. District Judge Peter Dorsey ruled against him, laying down a fundamental principle of American Law: "The question is not whether a rational basis has been shown for the policy chosen by the defendants," he said. "The plaintiff may have been disqualified unwisely, but he was not denied equal protection." Expecting a rational basis from our government? That's pretty extreme. (I'm told there are even stricter standards for the range of allowable IQs for judges in this district).

a DOG'S BeST FrieND

San Francisco is home to one of our nation's state-of-the-art animal shelters, providing "home-style" quarters for dogs and cats with Persian rugs, skylights, couches, tables, and, of course, TV sets. It was only a matter of time before someone noticed the facilities were superior to those offered to homeless humans. That individual was the local president of the Society for the Prevention of Cruelty to Animals, Richard Avanzino, who brought forth a plan to provide lodging for the homeless right alongside the dogs. His rationale: "It would give our dogs a chance to know what it would be like to have an overnight roommate ..." Not only could humans provide this valuable service, but they would get off the streets and gain a "dog buddy who will be their best friend overnight" (the post-AIDS version of the one-night stand). And yet another benefit: I'm told the shelter also provides toilet and obedience training ...

reVeNGe OF THe NerDS

In a major defense of traditional etiquette, Microsoft announced that in-person conversations (those occurring outside of computer networks) remain socially acceptable. Bob Muglia, a senior VP, explained why Microsoft annually hosts a face-to-face corporate summit for over a hundred top-level CEOs. According to Muglia, "Conversation is still the most efficient networking protocol that exists. There are still benefits to physical person-person interaction." Most interesting is the use of the word "still", as if it is only a matter of time before these primitive human units are surpassed. Why is it the leaders of the Information Age sound like such weak imitations of the Coneheads? Can't you just hear a robotic voice proclaiming, "Conversation ... an efficient networking protocol"?

KISS OF DEATH

A national telemarketing firm named Unitel discovered it had no choice but to shut down most of its phone operations in Frostburg, Maryland, and move them to Florida. Why? As their vice-president Ken Carmichael explained, the "culture and climate in Western Maryland is one of helping your neighbor and being empathetic and those sorts of things." (I particularly like the inclusion of the phrase "and those sorts of things," as if sanitary gloves should be worn when speaking of them.) This made Frostburg the first town in America to officially lose an industry because its citizens were too caring. I'm still waiting to learn which town in Florida was deemed suitable for Unitel's corporate culture.

A HISTORICAL FOOTNOTE

Students of comparative shallowness will want to put forth other decades as candidates in the search for complete cluelessness. I know the fifties have a lot going for them with Frankie Avalon and Annette Funicello's Beach Party movies. And who can forget California's Valley Girl subculture? But I'd like to direct your attention way back to my candidate, the slaveholding culture of the Deep South. Eugene D. Genovese, in his book *Roll, Jordan Roll*, describes an aristocratic culture where the "happy-go-lucky" slaves were treated as part of the family, their education through labor viewed as a "duty" and a "burden" to their Christian masters. When newly emancipated slaves deserted the plantations in droves, slave owners are said to have been genuinely traumatized by their lack of loyalty. As one "deserted" Southern belle put it, "I am beginning to lose confidence in the whole race."

Helpful Hints

Communication with the "depth challenged" presents numerous difficulties. Remember Plato's Allegory of the Cave — those who exit their insulated cocoons too quickly risk being blinded by the light. Among the groups who have attempted a more refined outreach to Middle America is the Barbie Liberation Organization. The BLO obtained several hundred Barbies and G.I. Joes and then performed a "stereotype-change" operation and placed the improved dolls back on store shelves. Customers discovered a deep-voiced Barbie who yelled, "Vengence is mine," and a G.I. Joe who demurely said, "Let's plan our dream wedding."

On another depth-challenged front, a successful stereotype reversal operation was performed by Native American students at the University of North Carolina. Intent on communicating how it feels to have one's identity used for sports team logos, the Native American students resorted to the simple tactic of renaming their basketball team. They are now the "Fighting Whities," complete with their own t-shirts and coffee mugs. Sometimes it's humorous pinpricks, not thunderous hammer blows, that can best penetrate defenses.

The Education Mall

A N ESTIMATED 10% OF a two-year-old's vocabulary now consists of brand names. By the age of three, most children can, thanks to the billions advertisers spend on their education, correctly identify over 100 brand names. Sit down with any group of kids and ask them to identify any advertising jingle you can think of, like "Mmmmm, good, mmmm good, that's what ..." Guaranteed, they will know it. Then ask the capital of a foreign country or who fought in World War I. What you'll get is silence. Let's face it, advertisers are now our kids' prime teachers. Joseph Quinlan, economist at Dean Whitter, says we now have "a global MTV generation." As an educator, I say let's sell them the farm and head off to the Bahamas. That's why this chapter deals with two aspects of education: professional and amateur (aka public) education.

TWO-WAY DISCOURSE

Child psychologists have been happily offering their services to advertisers, thus provoking concerns about the use of science to manipulate toddlers and preschoolers. John Mowen, president of the Society for Consumer Psychology, admitted the justness of these criticisms, but added a timely reminder. "What we don't want to see," he said, "are limitations on basic rights of corporations to free speech." (Their right to address children is spelled out in the constitution, isn't it?) Maybe we should have a special time when corporations could address our toddlers. We could call it "Monday, Tuesday, Wednesday, Thursday ..."

a place in the sun

A major cultural oversight was corrected when a group of advertising firms, lead by Brunico Communications, established the Golden Marble Awards to recognize achievements in children's advertising. Shelley Middlebrook, a vice-president with Brunico, explained the problem their group confronted: "A lot of children's ads don't win awards in conventional award shows because [they have] restrictions — they can't be too edgy because they are directed at children." (Translation: no thinly disguised S&M shots.) The annual Golden Marbles have helped "set a standard for children's ads." To appreciate how high the bar has been raised, you should know that the winner of the first Golden Marble was ... Hostess Twinkies.

baby wars

In a move that will help countless thousands of babies to internalize our culture's values, Kohlcraft Enterprises unveiled a line of Jeep SUV strollers. These are bigger, heavier-duty strollers with oversized wheels and a genuine Jeep logo, built to make sure that your baby will not come out second best in a collision with another toddler. Gail Smith, vice-president of marketing for Kohlcraft said, "It was a natural. It's following the whole SUV market itself." (Could she mean straight back into infantilism?) Besides ruggedness, *The Wall Street Journal* suggested, "Jeep wants its strollers to be something fathers, too, are comfortable with." And just how do you make fathers comfortable? In America you do it by adding fake chrome wheels, fake lug nuts, fake gearshifts, and fake steering wheels.

PreSCHOOL OUTreaCH

Cover Concepts Marketing Services had exciting news for their clients about the "captive audience" it had "penetrated": preschool toddlers. Cover Concepts followed up its success by delivering Calvin Klein notebooks to over 31,000 grade schools. They boast a network of 22,000 daycare centers where they deliver product samples, coupons, and coloring books in exchange for demographic data. That information is then sold to clients like McDonald's and Kellogg's to assist their targeted marketing campaigns. Cover Concepts has sparked the interest of eagle-eyed advertisers because, in its own words, it "offers a medium which penetrates an almost advertising-free environment." Just think of having thousands of little preschool minds all to yourself. Does that thought get ad people panting? Let me just say that the copy of *The Wall Street Journal* I read at the Elliott Bay Bookstore Café in Seattle had been drooled on right below the "advertising-free" phrase. Honest.

DeFeNDers OF CHILDHOOD

In Sweden, advertising aimed at children has long been banned. Sweden even proposed a similar ban for all the countries of the European Union. This move sparked a keen interest in children's rights by a coalition representing advertisers. Industry lobbyists were soon circulating a brochure that declared, "Children as consumers have a right to information about the products available to them. This right is enshrined in the UN Convention on the Child." If true, this means parents who interfere with their children's TV watching could be in danger of being listed as human rights violators. However, a little closer reading of the relevant Article 17, guaranteeing a child's access to information, has this nasty little clause about it being information of "social and cultural benefit to the child." ("Rats, foiled again," as Snidely Whiplash would say.)

NeW-aGe rOLe MODeLS

Children have been receiving more true-to-life scenes of violence thanks to a new genre of cartoons from Japan. These low-budget cartoons, like "Pokemon," "Dragon Ball Z," and "Digimon," are modeled on video games in which enemies are vanquished in gory detail. The high level of violence in these shows was defended by Joel Andryc, a VP at Fox, who pointed out that not only are kids used to this kind of violence, but there are benefits of such exposure. "The kids can relate to these characters," he said. "They see how someone can empower themselves and fight a monster and save the world." Presumably by following the example of Batman and, as in one episode, strangling the villain with a pole.

Power to the Little People

Public school districts were discovering they could raise money not only by accepting corporate sponsors, but also by offering their pupils up for market research. In numerous schools, children were being given the opportunity to participate in taste tests on cereals and focus groups right in their own classrooms. Robert Reynolds, president of Education Market Resources, explained that "the education marketplace [also known as "schools" in Oldspeak] offers tremendous potential to sell products, and to gain access to the youth market." In return, students' lives are enriched by the addition of another "educational process" to their curriculum. Mr. Reynolds stated that kids these days "love the feeling of empowerment, and we are empowering them, but we are doing it in a proper way." Can't you just see students bursting with pride at being allowed to help in a taste test? "Mom, Dad, I've been empowered."

Empowering Our Schools

Channel One, the news program that brings advertising to over eight million students in school, found a way to be participatory. No longer need students, teachers, and administrators be mere passive observers of the show. Channel One has been enlisting teachers and principals to help in marketing campaigns. Teachers, for example, were being engaged to help students write commercials for Snapple and design art for Pepsi vending machines. Principals were being sent coupons for Subway sandwiches that they can hand out to students. Said Channel One sales director

Martin Grant, participating in these ad campaigns is a way for teachers "to make the lesson relevant."

Answering actual criticism about turning teachers into marketing partners, CEO David Tanzer says that Channel One is "sensitive about turning schools into merchandisers, but it only runs promotional campaigns that benefit advertisers and students alike." "But Mr. Tanzer, aren't all ad campaigns of benefit to students?" asked Beaver Cleaver.

SUBVERSION IS EVERYWHERE

A cultural milestone of some sort was passed when 19-year-old Mike Cameron was suspended for wearing a Pepsi shirt on "Coke Day" at his high school in Evans, Georgia. Principal Gloria Hamilton described this heinous act as being disrespectful toward visiting Coke executives and as "being disruptive and trying to destroy the school picture." The school picture in question consisted of the loyal student body lined up dressed in Coke's red and white colors to spell the word "Coke." (At least they spelled it right.) This long-standing tradition of having school pictures in the form of product names has come about as companies like Coke and Pepsi have been buying up exclusive rights to whole cash-starved school districts. But rather than calling this "commercialization," Coke prefers, in the words of a spokesperson named Ms. Howe, to describe the practice as "developing a partnership with the schools."

NEW MATH

McGraw-Hill published a fine new mathematics textbook enriched with what appear to be advertisements for products like Nike runners, Kellogg's Cocoa Frosted Flakes, and M&M's. Neal Allen, spokesman for McGraw-Hill, said the brand names are used in the textbook only to give junior high school students "some examples they can appreciate." Thus in one problem we are asked how long a student named Will needs to save his allowance to purchase a pair of Nikes. The inclusion of brand names in the text and color photos of famous products is not considered advertising, however. That's because, says McGraw-Hill, no payments were made for them. Teacher-trainer Charlotte Mason presents an even stronger reason for allowing corporate symbols in public school texts. The students, she says, "don't even notice these things. They just see a book that is engaging." Thanks to whose conditioning?

UPSTAIrs, DOWNSTAIrs

Elite public schools across the nation have been saying good-bye to auctions and cookie sales as a means to raise funds. Public schools like Brookline High School in Boston are now simply raising $10 million permanent endowments from wealthy parents and alumni. This turn to large endowments came, said *The Wall Street Journal,* "in reaction to broad trends in school finance that have hit affluent districts like Brookline especially hard over the last decade." But the means chosen by these "hard-hit" schools to grow money has raised issues of fairness. Why should some public schools have piles of resources while others starve? "The equity issue, it's always going to come up," said Robert Markey, director of the Boston Latin School (a public school with a $13 million endowment). "That's why," he told the *Journal,* "we don't talk about it." And certainly not in front of the servants.

LET THEM STUDY CAKE DEPT.

In Cleveland, Ohio, Judy Kincaid was sent to jail for five days for a crime that is mushrooming: illegal school registration. The inner-city mother sent her five-year-old son to a kindergarten in the suburbs without authorization. Across the nation, inner-city parents have been resorting to subterfuge to escape overcrowded, under-funded city schools and enrolling their children in affluent suburban schools. To "protect" themselves, suburban districts have taken to hiring private investigators, offering bounties of up to $500 for identifying out-of-district illegal students, and have passed legislation making the use of a false address a misdemeanor. Fortunately, this raising of barriers to youth from poorer neighborhoods is being done with the best of intentions. As Elizabeth Fineberg, Superintendent of Schools in Morrisburg, Ohio, relates: "We're only staffed for the number of children we're supposed to have in the district. We don't want to have to give less to our children." Sadly, parents like Ms. Kincaid seem unable to appreciate the need to sacrifice for the good of "our" children.

SON OF reefer Madness

Buried somewhere in the welfare reform bill for 1996 were $250 million to teach children sexual abstinence. This money was to be given to local government programs teaching that sex outside of marriage "is likely to have harmful psychological and physical effects." How harmful, you ask? A joint report by the Applied Research Center and the Public Media Center presents these gems: In a funded educational video, a student asks, "What if I want to have sex before I get married?" An instructor answers, "Well, I guess you'll just have to prepare to die. And you'll probably take with you your spouse and your children." (Much worse than the blindness masturbation used to cause.) Another educational effort warns of the link between abortion and child abuse, stating that "after one has aborted a child, an individual loses instinctual control over rage." Fortunately, according to Amy Stevens of Friends of the Family, "These programs are not fear-based efforts ..." Thank heaven for small favors. To be on the safe side, do lock your doors securely to protect your family against possible roaming hordes of crazed women.

IMProving THe Past

In October of 1997, as a Halloween prank, a high school senior in Oneonta, New York, set off a bomb on a rooftop. Seventeen-year-old Ethan Brush was, of course, rightly suspended from school for the year. But an even worse fate was awaiting poor Ethan: the next spring, he found he had "disappeared" from the school yearbook. Not only did his name and photo not appear, but he had been carefully airbrushed out of a group photo that he had originally appeared in. This repicturing of history was defended by Principal Barry Gould on the grounds that appearing in the yearbook was a "privilege," and one that could be taken away. Some may find this unsettling, particularly students who are sure they were standing next to someone at the Chess club photo taking, for example, only to have the person next to them "disappeared." Could be years of therapy.

Even worse was the fate that befell high school senior Daniel Young in Madison, Connecticut. He'd shaved his head just before the yearbook portraits were to be taken at his school. His parents kindly intervened, just like England's royal family did for Prince William when it was discovered he hadn't given his all in the smile department at a royal wedding. Daniel's parents turned to photography company T. D. Brown to add nice curly hair to his photo and even improved the look of his clothing in the yearbook. You can imagine Daniel's excitement at having his parents pick out his hairstyle for him. Thanks to image-enhancing software, any customer can enjoy a Stalin-like privilege, rewriting his or her life and being assured of a perpetual happy face for as little as $19. Not only pimples and braces, but entire people can be removed from group photos for a mere $200. Is this falsifying reality? Photographer Craig Brown (of the same company) has an answer: "What we're doing is giving control back to the customer." Or the parents, or whoever wants to exercise control.

Bureaucracy appreciation 101

Public furor over the suspensions of two boys, age six and seven, for sexual harassment and then a 13-year-old girl for possessing Midol caused many people to miss the nearly flawless performances of our school bureaucracies. When seven-year-old De'Andre Dearinge of New York City came home with a letter from school, he thought he was being rewarded for a good day. It turned out to be an announcement of his suspension listing as the reason — "Sexual Harassment." That was it. No more explanation. Perfect Kafka. Kissing fit the official definition, so case closed. Later New York school officials said they would "review" their policies, using, ironically, the same word employed by Napoleon after Waterloo.

In Ohio, following the breakup of a notorious Midol drug ring, school spokesperson Joy Paolo admitted their drug policies did not distinguish between legal and illegal drugs (nitpicking) and said,

"We're real comfortable with our policy and it's pretty much in line with what most districts do." Can't argue with that strong defense. Whether the "comfortable" district will follow through with a strong "Just Say No" campaign against aspirin was left unclear, as were the contents of the drug rehab program for Midol users.

"a rose by any other name ..."

Prep schools, to justify their high tuition, are under tremendous pressures to land students in Ivy League colleges. This has led to a few problems. For example, at the Shady Side Academy in Pittsburgh, the director of college counseling was forced to step down after marking an "H" for honors on the transcripts of a dozen student transcripts. Unfortunately, the school did not have honors classes. Shady Side's president, Peter Kountz, minimized this apparent transgression. "We didn't distort any numbers or change grades," he said. "We described courses in an enhanced way." This helps explains why private schools provide such a solid foundation for corporate and government careers.

Helpful Hints

Corporate and government officials love to receive awards, but they hate receiving nagging letters. That's why they have paper shredders. So the next time you spot cutting-edge advances in Newspeak, you might want to consider showcasing the achievement with an award and sharing it with your community. For example, after the Golden Marble Awards for children's advertisements were started, a parents group began presenting the "Have You Lost Your Marbles?" Awards to noteworthy marketers to kids. These honors can be found at www.commercialexploitation.com.

Also, the National Council of Teachers of English issues yearly "Doublespeak Awards" to deserving politicians (www.ncte.org). The number of fun categories is endless. With all the drug testing today, what could be more natural than a Best Urine Award? Can't you see Costco proudly displaying such a trophy?

Class Frontiers

T HE EXPLOSION OF wealth among the affluent led to a virtual renaissance of conspicuous consumption, status striving, and uniformed guards to keep out the unwashed. In biology it's known as species differentiation. I think people underestimate the hard work it takes to become "rich" in the social sense. It takes concentrated practice to learn how to talk down to people who may be much smarter and talented. Guilt-free snobbery is not innate — it's an accomplishment. Fortunately, psychologists have rushed in to help affluent clients deal with "sudden-wealth syndrome," a discovery that has led, I'm told, to their own sudden-wealth syndrome.

OUT OF THE CLOSET

While donations for charitable causes were stagnating, the sale of luxury goods took off beginning in the mid-nineties. Dan Phillips, editor of the *Robb Report*, stated that the "luxury industry is alive and well. It's acceptable to be well off again." Conspicuous consumption has its ups and downs. Isaac Lagnado, publisher of *The Tactical Retail Monitor*, recalled that in "the 80's there was a progressive buildup of wealth and the need to flaunt it." This primal need to display your BMWs does undergo periods of repression as occurred in the early 1990s when, reported Mr. Lagnado, with all the downsizing there was actually "embarrassment at flaunting prosperity." (Unbelievable but true.) Can't you just picture wealthy grandparents describing the "hardships" they endured during those times, just as an earlier generation once spoke of having to walk miles through the snow to get to school. Fortunately, the shift of wealth to the already wealthy has, according to Cornell economist Robert Frank, "shifted the standards of acceptable consumption levels" — America's version of moral progress.

COMMUNICATING WITH YOUR HIRED HELP 101

The booming economy for the upper classes and the new availability of illegal immigrants have fueled a rebirth of household servants. Over 1.8 million people now work as housekeepers, cooks, nannies, gardeners, and chauffeurs in a field expanding at five times the rate of overall job growth. Fortunately, a book appeared in the nick of time to help employers manage at least their Latino helpers. It's entitled *Household Spanish: How to Communicate With Your Spanish Employees* and is written by William C. Harvey. This book is chock-full of Spanish phrases essential for good relations, phrases like "Bring the dustpan," "Please use soap," and "Don't pour grease down the garbage disposal." You can learn how to ask prospective helpers whether they have been a bellhop, busboy, pool cleaner, or dishwasher. Then you can tell them about your career as an architect, doctor, or lawyer, etc. Among my favorite phrases are "How long are you planning to stay in the USA?" and "There's so much to do." The author even provides helpful advice like this: "Commands are practical and easy to use, but don't overuse them." So true. As an added bonus, the book provides the all-important phrase "You're fired" ("Usted esta despedido"). Invaluable.

PLEASANTVILLE

According to the Community Associations Institute, an estimated ten million Americans live in what are called "master-planned" suburban communities. These have been designed around the needs of mobile, affluent families who want safe, tightly controlled environments filled with like-minded people. These suburban oases offer strict covenants that prohibit a whole range of "questionable" practices, creating restrictions almost as exciting as book bannings. In Houston's "Woodlands" community, houses may be painted only in approved colors, garbage cans may not be visible, barbecue grills may not be located in the front yard (very tacky), garage sales are forbidden, and bug-zapper lights may not be placed more than six feet off the ground. Two residents, who mercifully will be left nameless, are quoted as defending this high level of conformity because it is there "to protect our own interests." (Particularly the bug-zapper light rule). And there is evidence these covenants work very well: 50% of the violations are reported by neighbors. Sorry, no statistics are available on the number of parents turned in by their children.

Top honors must go to the town of San Juan Capistrano in California. They've banned the display of clotheslines in their community. Once it was sexuality that our Puritan ethics forbade. Now it's any reminders of our grandparents' less affluent lifestyles. As a public service, here is my list of Cultural Artifacts Deserving Banishment By Any Self-respecting Upper Class Community:

1. Hand-powered lawnmowers,
2. Black-and-white televisions,
3. Manual garage doors,
4. Anything with a Kmart sticker,
5. Typewriters,
6. Jell-O,
7. Meatloaf,
8. Houses without visible servant entries.

HaPPY ENDINGS

In California's Orange County, communities have been addressing the more serious problem of children from households with modest stock portfolios invading wealthier enclaves under the guise of public education. For example, upscale residents of Coto de Caza fought the Capistrano School District over plans to locate a public school in their district. According to *The Wall Street Journal*, "homeowners said a public school threatened their private community." The happy "compromise": a K-3 school limited to the children of Coto de Caza residents. The real trendsetter may be Orange County's Silver Creek Country Club. Faced with a similar intrusion of merely middle-class children, they found a developer willing to donate land to the local school district on the border of the community. The result: the construction of a Silver Oak Elementary School with two entrances, one for the "outside" children and one for the children of Silver Creek members (who quite naturally are accorded priority in admission).

NEW ENTITLEMENTS

Just as the rich have been getting richer, so have the children of the rich. Child support awards in divorce cases have been soaring as courts have gained a finer appreciation of the needs of wealthy children. In one divorce case in Pennsylvania, a Ms. Amy Karp was able to convince the court her four children needed $23,266 a month child support from their father, millionaire investor Michael Karp, so they would not feel "second-class" with her. Presumably the offspring of poor parents lack this sensitivity to feeling second-class and so can get by with child support measured in hundreds or tens of dollars per month. Ms. Karp's lawyers cited another Pennsylvania divorce case where it had been decided that rich children not only should have, but also were entitled to, "good restaurants, good hotels, good shows, and good camps." Thank heavens that court restrained itself from following the same logic and determining that poor children were entitled to bad restaurants, bad hotels, bad shows, and bad camps.

As we move up the social food chain, we find children's needs expanding. How much does it cost to support a four-year-old child in the wealthiest neighborhoods of America? These figures from the divorce settlement between billionaire Ronald Perelman and Patricia Duff will intrigue future anthropologists. The lawyers for Ms. Duff argued her four-year-old child was entitled to the following monthly budget: travel — $9,953, clothing — $3,175, recreation — $3,585, dining out — $1,450, and hired help — $30,098. In addition, $350,000 was requested to redecorate the child's room and, did I forget, funds were naturally requested for a pediatrician to accompany the child while traveling. As the lawyer for Ms. Duff explained, "These numbers speak for themselves." Volumes.

A totally unrelated statistic: the United Nations estimates approximately 35,000 children die each day from malnutrition. (Forgive my lapse in etiquette.)

"ain't GOING DOOr-TO-DOOr NO MOre ..."

A cultural milestone of sorts was passed when a community stepped forth to rid its streets of Girl Scout cookie sellers. The exclusive town of Medina on the shores of Lake Washington, home to a certain William Gates, voted to amend its solicitation code to effectively bar young Scouts and Brownies from selling cookies door-to-door. In a classic win-win solution, the city decided to leave charitable groups both the right to solicit in Medina's neighborhoods and the "right" to get entangled in red tape. Ten-year-old cookie sellers just have to fill out an application, purchase a $15 license, wear a photo ID, register any vehicles, and, best of all, have a criminal background check. No more than you'd expect to enter any foreign country. (A neighborhood where the average house costs $868,100 is rated foreign where I come from.)

If you are like me, the thought of children coming into the community without criminal background checks is a little scary. On the other hand, just imagine the pride you'd feel if your young Cub Scout or Brownie passed Medina's criminal test. I'd be bragging for weeks. My own neighborhood is trying to follow Medina's example.

In our case, it's a matter of getting the local street gangs to fill out applications before they "solicit" us. It hasn't worked very well.

Medina City Manager Doug Schulz said the law was not aimed at the Girl Scouts or even charitable groups. The law, he said, was intended for "strong-arm salesmen" and "pesky peddlers" (at least those who aren't residents, I should add). However, the new ordinance was, said Mr. Schulz, "crafted in a way that does not discriminate." There is good news for you bleeding-heart liberals. Mr. Schulz pointed out that Girl Scouts may be able to avoid the red tape because "Girl Scouts typically go out to people and homes they know." This means "it would be up to the home-owner to decide whether the solicitor is a guest to their house and therefore not subject to the restrictions." He did not say what Girl Scouts should do if the homeowner determines they are not guests. Fortunately, we have some advice for young cookie sellers:

1. Smile real big.
2. Run as fast as you can while consulting your Scout manual under "Emergencies."
3. Ask mommy or daddy for a lawyer's phone number.

SOCIAL CLIMBING 101

Status-conscious moviegoers in many cities have been offered new choices in theater complexes run by Cineplex Odeon, United Artists, and General Cinema. For an additional eight dollars or so they can avoid having to mix with the unwashed masses. They can now go directly to private viewing rooms, receive valet parking, be personally escorted by a concierge, order drinks from a waiter, and use a private bathroom. *The Wall Street Journal* described this trend as "a way to express the affluence." But unlike luxury boxes at sports stadiums, where seats can approach the thousand-dollar range, the movie theaters have, says the *Journal*, "discovered affordable snobbery." It allows people of simple means to publicly parade their social importance, if only for a few hours. The *Journal*, of course, was able to find a telling phrase to describe this trend, referring to it as "the democratization of status." Sounds a little like having a genuine Xerox copy of a photo of Bill Gates' mansion.

The need to build so many luxury boxes is viewed as one of the unfortunate results of the prejudices of an earlier generation of architects. Steven Wolff, president of AMS Planning and Research, noted that after World War II there was a "democratization of the architecture," leaving us with cavernous halls with seats all on one level. This was apparently a short-lived aberration. The return to luxury boxes and white-gloved servants is viewed as a welcome relief. Peter Ventimialia, a vice-president with Bell Atlantic, stated, "It's genteel, it's more intimate; it appeals to a different sort of client." Equality is fine for those who like that sort of thing, but refined tastes require a bit more.

FrIENDLY SKIES

Airlines have been responding to the growing gap between the rich and the rest of us by, in the words of *Business Week*, "making the plush seats even plusher" and catering more to the needs of their business passengers. Socially conscious airlines like TWA squeezed coach seats 15% closer so that first-class passengers could enjoy more space and seating. (Coach class passengers will presumably enjoy more ... togetherness?) Mark Shields of Mercer Management Consulting said that "increasingly people will be handled in subtly but importantly different ways." Much of the credit goes to computer software that allows airline employees to target "profitable" customers and so meet their needs better. Let me see if I get this: if wealthy passengers are going to be treated better, then I'm going to be treated "subtly" like what?

SHOrTaGES HIT EVEN THE aFFLUENT

"Lots of wealthy people won't get what they want for Christmas," reported *The Wall Street Journal*. The shortage of hotel accommodations at elite resorts was sending shudders through our nation's country clubs. Increasingly, rich couples were finding it impossible to find space for their winter vacations at exclusive hideaways in the Caribbean and the Mediterranean unless they make reservations a year in advance. Then they faced the hardship of having to "scramble" for a limited number of first-class airline seats. And as if that were not enough, many arrive at their destination and then run into the type of problem encountered by two New York investment bankers who flew to the secluded Casa de Campo in the Dominican Republic only to discover the rooms didn't come with maids! These shortages in luxury accommodations have struck the rich hard because, as yacht broker Ann-Willis White was quoted as saying, "Most of our clients aren't accustomed to being told no." By the strangest of coincidences, that's the same problem faced by teachers of five-and six-year-olds in elementary schools.

Wall Street angst

Tax lawyers for the wealthy voiced concerns that their ingenuity in keeping superwealthy clients from paying taxes could trigger a backlash. Wall Street has become so adept at mining tax loopholes that David Bradfore, economist at Princeton, admitted that "anyone sitting on a pot of money today probably is not paying capital gains taxes." Robert Willens, director of Lehman Brothers, said, "I worry there is a growing perception that these tax techniques are only available to the wealthy few ..." Note his worry is limited to the *perception* of unfairness and as opposed to extending to the reality of it. But not everyone on Wall Street was worried. Bankers Trust happily offered seminars on the "wonderful window of opportunity" open to investors to avoid any capital gains taxes — under the slogan "You can have your cake and eat it too." Nice literary touch.

Going Native

Directors of arts and civic organizations were discovering that self-sacrifice pays off when it comes to fundraising. Richard Koshalek, director of the Museum of Contemporary Art in Los Angeles, gave up much of his personal time because of the pressing need to be around wealthy people every single day. "You can't just ask them for money out of the blue," he said. "You have to be one of them." In the trade, this is called "living the life," and it means that arts and civic leaders have been developing higher "lifestyle requirements" (i.e., $25,000 entertainment allowances,

BMWs, and housing that will allow them to entertain the wealthy as equals). The advantage of being a social chameleon, said Mr. Koshalek (who would prefer other metaphors, I believe), is that "in meeting rich donors, I can talk about what they like. I travel where they travel, read what they read." Plus he can save on the expense of maintaining a personal identity as well.

SMALL AIN'T BEAUTIFUL NO MORE

If there is a Hell for environmentalists who've preached about consuming less and living lightly upon the planet, it will be wallpapered with a series of ads for the Lincoln Town Car. The Lincoln magazine ads feature the "spacious comfort," "distinctive design," and "quiet elegance" we would expect from a luxury car. But this stylish sedan has attitude as well. As the ad's headline proclaims, "This should finally put an end to all that 'less is more' nonsense." And then Lincoln poses the critical question: "Whose idea was this 'less is more' business anyway? Certainly not ours." Most certainly not. Lincoln knows what it proudly stands for, its raison d'être: "Because having it all is what this car is all about." It must feel great being all the way out of the closet. Just be careful and don't run over any of the peasants on the way out of the showroom.

SILVER SPOON DEPT.

Citibank launched a crusade to help the children of wealthy parents. In a full-page ad in *The New York Times Magazine*, Citibank ran a probing interview on "Raising Children of Affluence" with Peter White, the director of their Family Advisory Practice. Mr. White was asked, "Is being born into wealth a burden?" You'll be reassured to know that "it doesn't have to be. But it comes with its own set of complexities." That's why Citibank stands prepared to help affluent clients deal with the problems of offspring who may never have to work. The interview ends with an invitation for readers: "To have your own dialogue with Peter, call 212.559.0446." Give "Peter" a call. I suggest asking Peter if he'd be willing to donate one coffee break to a dialogue on problems of the poor. That's 212.559.0446.

Helpful Hints

It's considered quite difficult to penetrate the cozy cocoons of the overprivileged, to aid them in feeling how others in the world must live. Sometimes role-playing can act as an eye-opener. For example, the hunger organization Oxfam annually sponsors dinner parties that mirror real world conditions. Guests enter a lottery to determine at which table they will eat. A few "winners" go to the First World table in the center of the room where they are treated to a lavish feast with more than they can ever swallow. A larger group is ushered to surrounding Second World tables where they can eat a simple but nutritious meal. A much larger group is herded to a wider circle of Third World tables where they are fed a small bowl of rice. The remaining people are served nothing and must beg for their food. Very educational. I recommend rigging the results so the "right" people get the right begging bowls. You can find Oxfam at www.oxfamamerica.org.

Ad Nation

*T*HE *WALL STREET JOURNAL* once asked, "Is the market penetrating too deeply into American life?" I'll be damned if it didn't turn out to be just a rhetorical question. *Business Week* estimates Americans are bombarded with about 3,000 commercial messages a day (counting all media), each ad drumming in one simple message: "Consume, consume consume ..." By way of comparison, consider the conditioning of the population envisioned in Aldous Huxley's *Brave New World*. His "controllers" played recorded slogans to sleeping children — 200 repetitions a night of the same slogan. That is bush league compared to the job our advertisers are doing today. Huxley's "controllers" couldn't get in the front door of a modern ad agency. We're rightfully number one in mass conditioning because so many advertisers leave no stone unturned.

AD AGENCY PHOBIAS

In their search for emotionally compelling ideas advertisers are running into a roadblock. It's getting harder and harder to reach consumers who are hit by an estimated 300 commercial TV messages a day. David Lubars, an ad executive with the Omnicom Group with an enviable literary touch, complained that consumers "are like roaches — you spray them and spray them and they get immune after a while." A truly humbling simile. Meanwhile, to get around this resistance, advertisers have long relied on focus groups to get at consumers' real feelings about products. But now even this approach is failing because, said *The Wall Street Journal*, over-saturated consumers "display an alarming tendency to re-gurgitate ad-world lingo ..." Ask and people will now say they like Sanka because of its "full-bodied aroma." Look at what happens when you do your job too well. In the quest for spontaneous or "naked" subconscious reactions upon which to base new ad campaigns, researchers have been turning to scanning eyeball movements and using hypnosis. It's a tough job getting past the conditioning your own ads have inflicted.

INNer CITY BeaUTIFICaTION

With limits on the numbers of outdoor billboards, inner city buildings have seen an explosion of advertising on their walls. Ads occupying up to 10,000 square feet can command rental fees of up to $60,000 a month. With such a profit potential, new buildings are being designed with external walls already reserved for billboards. To critics who questioned whether every building in a city need be covered with ads, Lee Wagman, the CEO of TrizecHahn Development Corp., had an answer that signaled an important cultural sea change. Pointing to the $600 million retail/hotel/entertainment complex his company was building in Los Angeles, Wagman noted that the "project would look out of place if it didn't incorporate commercial messages." Right-thinking people might think him abnormal. But his statement simply reflects the famous opinion expressed by Matthew Smith, CEO of the Federal Sign Company in Atlanta: "A city with no signs is a city with no personality." A uniquely American per-spective. I'm told he had ancient Athens and Rome in mind as his models of blandness.

HOW TO advertise your assault guns

There was a bright side to the ruling by the California Supreme Court protecting gunmakers from being sued: the trial helped showcase the creative advertising efforts of America's assault gun industry. No matter what your views are on people running around the streets with Saturday Night Specials, we can all appreciate quality advertising. The court ruled in a 5-1 decision that the victims of gun violence cannot sue gun manufacturers for the carnage their products inflict. Crucial to the case was the claim that a Miami-based firm named Navegar used advertising deliberately targeted to people prone to violence. This impression was arrived at simply because Navegar advertised their guns' resistance to fingerprints and their compatibility with silencers. People are so touchy today.

The TEC-DC9 semi-automatic pistol produced by Navegar has become the weapon of choice amongst mass-killers. It was one of the guns used at Columbine High School, and was featured exclusively by Gian Luigi Ferri when he went on a shooting rampage in 1993 in San Francisco, killing eight. The compact pistol offers all the advantages of a submachine gun without the embarrassment of having to carry a violin case. Navegar's brochures praise it for being "as tough as your toughest customer," as having a "gutsy performance." And: "It's fun. It's affordable. And it's hot." They tell us. By far my favorite of the Navegar ad jingles, unearthed by the Violence Policy Center, is the following: "Only your imagination limits your fun." What a literate and colorful sentence. Picture yourself dancing through a field of wildflowers with your assault gun ...

Unfortunately, two of Navegar's ad claims produced a small bit of confusion. The gunmaker noted in one advertisement, cited at the trial, that their assault gun had "excellent resistance to fingerprints." Some people have interpreted this as a clear enticement to criminals. I, on the other hand, am able to see Navegar's real intent. They obviously are just trying to encourage cleanliness. Would Pierce be caught dead with his gun covered with greasy fingerprints? No. A similar misinterpretation occurred when the Miami gunmaking firm promoted their threaded barrel, announcing it allowed for the easy attachment of a silencer. Critics leapt to the conclusion that Navegar was targeting potential assassins, ignoring the possibility that they were merely interested in reducing noise pollution. I mean, who wants to hear drive-by shootings? It's a nuisance.

CHarLIE GETS HIP

Reaching twentysomethings has proven a challenge to Madison Avenue. Given this age group's media savvy cynicism, many corporations have turned to young upstart ad agencies like Gyro Worldwide, who specialize in projecting a "cool, hip sensibility." (I'm not the only one who projects it.) Gyro's leader, Steven Grasse, first gained notoriety in 1993 for an ad for Zipper Head clothes displaying a picture of mass murderer Charles Manson with the message: "Everyone has the occasional urge to go wild and do something completely outrageous." In the resulting uproar over the ad, Gyro lost accounts and Grasse thought his business was through. But now for the rest of the story ... Viacom, R.J. Reynolds, and Coca-Cola immediately recognized the "hip sensibility" displayed in the Manson ad and hired the agency. Since then Gyro has rapidly grown and even branched out into publishing a soft-porn magazine called *Hollywood Highball*. Said the now wealthy Mr. Grasse: "It's cool. It helps our image."

GEN X aDS GO NeGaTIVE

Business Week reported that commercials aimed at twentysomethings have been taking on an even harder edge. Increasingly, ads have been emphasizing the raw struggle for existence against a background of scarcity. Examples are ads for the soft drink Surge, depicting Gen X'ers racing up a muddy hill for one bottle of Surge. Or there is the popular slogan for Twix candy bars taken from the Republican platform: "Two for me, none for you." Advertisers say that kids who absorb some 20,000 commercials a year are immune to kinder and gentler appeals. But are advertisers sending a bad message to our youth? Answering this question is

William Oberlander, creative director at Kirschenbaum Bond & Partners, who wins our award for honesty: "No one's really worrying about what it's teaching impressionable youth. Hey, I'm in the business of convincing people to buy things they don't need." That about says it all. Thanks William.

Drawing the line

The Center for Media Education issued a scurrilous report charging our liquor and tobacco companies with creating websites designed to appeal to teenagers. Fortunately, the PR reps for those companies were quick to set the record straight. First up to bat to defend the cartoon- and game-filled sites was Elizabeth Board of the Distilled Spirits Council. "Just because you have games and are interactive does not mean you are targeting children," she argued. So true. Next, Seagram spokeswoman Bevin Gore said their website and its Captain Morgan character "appealed to hip, irreverent consumers of legal drinking age and above." Likewise, Jack Dougherty of Budweiser reported their website was "designed to attract the same people as Bud TV ads — 21- to 34-year-old males." Apparently critics have ignored the abilities of these companies to appeal to the hip sensibilities of 21-year-olds while leaving their 20-year-old friends in the dark. And these sites even have signs warning underage youth they cannot enter. Teenagers tell me they always obey such posted notices.

Beyond Upscale

The old-fashioned catalog may be making way for a new format, the "magalog." Upscale merchants like Ambercrombie & Fitch have discovered they need more than the conventional catalog to communicate their message, so they have been publishing combined magazine/catalogs that intermix fascinating articles on topics like "How to Look Cool" with displays of merchandise and advertising from other companies. The advantage? It "sells the Ambercrombie lifestyle." Those who have yet not attained the Ambercrombie lifestyle have a chance to learn its rudiments. And why would other companies want to advertise in these magalogs?

Steven Kornajiek, overseer of Nieman Marcus's "book" explains that their readers "have a very high taste level and the psychographics are right: They are proven shoppers." Who wouldn't want those words of praise on their resume?

PHILLIP MOrris DOes "THe WOMaN THING"

Phillip Morris's feminine cancer stick division has gone into music. Virginia Slims produced a series of CDs showcasing up-and-coming female vocalists in what critics describe as an end run around advertising restrictions. Au contraire, said event marketer Mary Jo Gennaro, "It's all part of Virginia Slim's tradition of providing opportunities for women to showcase their talents and interests." Such venerable traditions cannot be ignored. First online to be promoted was Martha Brynes, the star of the soap opera *As the World Turns*. She was sent on a nationwide tour with her new CD, *The Woman Thing*, available free with the purchase of two packages of Virginia Slims. Ms. Brynes, a non-smoker, said, "I don't feel I'm being used ... The goal of the label is to bring women into a positive light, period." Thank heavens there are no base materialistic motives! Interestingly, Virginia Slims is being marketed as a men's cigarette in Korea where they apparently have an underdeveloped sense of "The Woman Thing."

FaCING THe CHaLLeNGe

A shocking research finding was presented at the 88th convention of the Association of National Advertisers devoted to "Branding the Future." Scott Bedberry, a marketing VP with Starbucks, told the assembled ad executives that today, "Consumers don't truly believe there's a huge difference between products"! How to respond to such traitorous notions? Encourage employees to make real changes? Hire scientists to design new products? No. The key, says Mr. Bedberry, is to "establish emotional ties" between brands and consumers. Fortunately, this is a mounting trend. Carl Pascarella, CEO of VISA USA, proclaimed the good news that "name-brand products have recaptured the hearts and minds of consumers." Now that we are all breathing a sigh of relief, there is this advice from John Haynes of American Express on how to solidify the all-important brand-customer bond. Using a definition of the term *dialogue* that I'm unfamiliar with, Haynes tells advertisers to "create and sustain a dialogue with your customer." Fortunately, I have a list of institutions filled with people willing to "dialogue" with their TV screens.

SPONSOreD CONVersaTIONS

The British, of all people, beat us to a new advertising frontier (which is so embarrassing). An advertising firm called Impact FCA was paying one hundred cabbies in London to insert a plug for Siemens, a Germany-based global communications firm, into their regular banter. The cabbies were paid an undisclosed sum to inject three main selling points for the Siemens mobile phone into their conversation. "They must mention German technology, a small but powerful battery, and the ability to upgrade the telephone for more services," reported *The London Times*, all without alerting passengers to the fact they are being pitched. Why waste perfectly good conversations when they could be put to commercial use? This could even put our homeless to work: "Spare change? And have you tried the new Remmington razor?"

When I first wrote about this story I actually wrote the following sentence: "If successful, look for bartenders and waitresses next." I sat back and chortled at how witty I'd become. Two years later it was learned that tobacco companies in the U.S. were doing exactly that — turning bartenders and waitresses into walking commercials. Companies like Brown & Williamson were spending up to $30 million a year to make sure that bartenders gave the right advice about smoking and had free samples to giveaway. PR firm KBA Marketing, for example, had 450 employees whose sole job was to visit, on behalf of R.J. Reynolds, some 2,000 bars a week. Bar owners received from $2,000 to $50,000 a year to promote a particular brand while bartenders received perks like ski vacations for sharing their newfound opinions. You may remember how actors in the movie *The Truman Show* introduced commercials into scenes of everyday life. Once again reality beats fiction.

FINAL SANCTUARY

Yet another country, Sweden, beat the United States to the punch in the newest advertising frontier: telephone calls. Forty thousand customers of a phone company named Gratistelefon Svenska get to hear a 10-second ad during every three minutes they spend on the phone, as does anyone talking to them. Not only do dull conversationalists get their experience on the phone jazzed up, customers also receive free phone service. Gratistelefon executives say the service has succeeded beyond all expectations thanks to one secret: the use of "intelligent software." New customers must fill in exhaustive questionnaires, which allow them to be targeted with pinpoint accuracy by advertisers. Co-founder Carl Ander proudly declares, "If a diaper company wants to reach households with babies, we can do it." Not only can they properly target customers and help end their dirty diaper woes, but they can promise their advertisers "the full attention of users." No need to worry about inattentive slobs turning the page and ignoring ads. Gratistelefon can insert your company's message right into the middle of people's most intimate moments. Can't you imagine someone proposing marriage on the phone: "Darling, I want to ... [voice cuts in] tell you about the new improved Dutch Cleanser." We never need be separated from our commercial fixes again.

NEW, IMPROVED MOON

No longer would the moon be wasted on young lovers if advertisers Gary Betts and Malcolm Green have their way. The two London ad executives announced plans to turn the moon into a giant billboard. After consulting with NASA scientists, the two believe they have a feasible plan for projecting corporate logos onto the moon's surface using reflected sunlight from two large umbrella-shaped mirrors. In the scientific community, the major debate seemed to be over how and not over whether to project brand names onto the moon. French scientists have reportedly come up with a cheaper way to get corporate logos into space using reflecting satellites. Meanwhile, the news agency Reuters treated this as a step up for the lowly moon, adding that now "the moon could be more than just a part of the solar system."

Take Back the Night

Bozell Worldwide, the producers of those milk ads featuring moo-staches, produced a fine memo for their new employer, the liquor industry. They suggested the industry spend $20 to $40 million on cable TV ads in a campaign to "own the night." Bozell was hired by the Distilled Spirits Council to help stem a 40% drop in hard-liquor consumption since 1980 that had led the industry to shelve their self-imposed ban on TV advertising. All of which poses the question of how a cutting-edge ad agency can skirt around a call to Americans to get drunk. Bozell's answer: a "communications" effort to "rebuild occasion frequency." Spokeswoman Judy Blatman defended the industry's ad campaign by noting that this is "a highly competitive industry and we are just trying to compete on an equal footing with beer and wine." It's only fair they have an equal role in rebuilding America's "occasion frequency."

Final Barriers Dept.

Consumer expert Robert M. McMath had some timely warnings about the difficulties of extending brand names into new territory or forms. For example, in the 1980s, the Block Drug Company introduced Efficol Cough Whip, a cough suppressant and decongestant in an aerosol can. But consumers couldn't reconcile the dessert topping form with its role as medicine, so it failed. On the other hand, by the 1990s, consumers were ready to accept Starbucks coffee in an ice cream bar form. Mr. McMath concludes from this that "narrow package association barriers may eventually break down, but it is going to take a great deal more investment and creative effort by innovative product manufacturers to make it happen." Meanwhile, we can all help, I presume, by examining our souls to see if we have any remaining "narrow package association barriers" that still need to be dismantled.

"WHaT'S THaT IN THe SKY ...?"

Many of the comic book superheroes from our youth were being put to work not only to keep our streets safe but to help sell more American products. Spiderman was helping to sell Castrol Motor Oil while Iron Man promoted Phillip Morris Altoid Mints, and Superman did double duty pitching the Jeep Cherokee and American Express. Advertisers like the superheroes because they work cheap and have instant recognition. Although this may sound like yet another case of commercialization gone out of control, there has been good news. The owner of these superheroes, DC Comics, which in turn is owned by Time Warner, recognized that their "global brands" (as they refer to Batman and friends) would suffer from being overexploited. According to DC Comics publisher Paul Levitz, "Superman and Batman have to each stand for a certain set of things. You try to preserve the magic." Now Superman will fight for truth, justice, and the American Express Way. A modest change.

DeeP THOUGHTS

There's always great excitement when news comes that Hallmark has unveiled a new series of greeting cards. But 1998's announcement was more somber. Recognizing that the holiday season can be painful for those who have recently lost a loved one, Hallmark responded with a series of Christmas "Messages of Comfort" for the grief-stricken. This was timely, for, as *The Wall Street Journal* informed us, "Such people are a consumer niche that corporate marketers in the past have approached indirectly, if at all." Imagine being a consumer left alone with no companies vying to sell to you? Pretty lonely. Fortunately, greeting card companies "now recognize the potential for such a category as tremendous." There is no shortage of profit to be mined yet out of grief. In fact, said the *Journal*, "the category could hold potential for other industries, say travel." Maybe we should all start chasing hearses?

eMPOWerMeNT UPDaTe

Microsoft has announced plans for a series of interactive "shop operas" created by Hollywood producer Bob Bejan. Every day visitors to these projected shows would be able to interact in dramas with characters drawn from shopping catalogs produced by marketers like Victoria's Secret and J. Crew. With a click of the mouse, participants would be able to alter the story line, make purchases, and "change the colors of a model's teddy." With a little more mouse-clicking you could even get a "sexy model to wiggle in her lingerie and describe her romantic designs on a hunky male counterpart." And in a stroke of creative genius, Mr. Bejan even proposed to let visitors' purchases determine the story line. (How true to life.) All of this was part of a larger vision of interactive media. "We are choreographing your experience," Mr. Bejan said. "We are manipulating you to the point where we are maximizing your feeling of empowerment." Imagine all the wasted empowerment running about unmaximized.

FrieNDLY FirearMS

The National Shooting Sports Foundation launched an ad campaign to help Americans think of guns as sporting equipment. Doug Painter, of the ad firm Porter Novelli, pointed out that for many urban Americans, guns were associated with "crime and violence as opposed to hunting and skeet shooting." (The inner-city kids I surveyed were ignorant not only of skeet shooting but of polo and cricket as well). To correct this abysmal lack of knowledge, the NSSF has come up with a thought-provoking slogan to explain why guns are so safe when used properly. Shown in its ads against the backdrop of a Ruger shotgun are the words "The very fact that it can be dangerous is what makes it safe." Great slogan. We can only wonder if this will be extended to help promote other seemingly dangerous activities like crab fishing in the Bering Sea, jumping from 20-story buildings, or wrestling alligators.

Helpful Hints

Our billboard industry does a wonderful job of communicating about numerous products — everywhere. But sometimes citizens feel a need to "improve" outdoor ads or engage them in a dialogue, particularly after the Supreme Court opened the doors for free expression by tobacco and liquor companies near schools. Fortunately, the Billboard Liberation Front has posted a wonderful how-to manual on the Internet called "The Art and Science of Billboard Improvement" (www.billboardliberation.com). Among their recommendations: Always strive to maintain professional standards when making improvements. Be sure to match fonts and colors. Try using software like Adobe Pagemaker with its "tiling" feature, which allows printing out extra large improvements (or use the "enlarge" feature on copiers). Mount your work on heavy pattern paper and then glue it to the target billboard with rubber cement. Be sure to photograph your work and share it on the Internet.

Media-speak

The growth of the media has resembled the plot of Agatha Christie's *Ten Little Indians*, in which one houseguest after another is murdered on a secluded estate until only one remains. With the merger of Time Warner and America Online, we're down to about six multinational corporations controlling most of the flow of information around the world. Some view this in a positive light. For example, investment banker Porter Bibb of Bertelsmann A. G. (the purchasers of Random House), observes that the media have been "undergoing radical changes that could transform the business from the last great cottage industry into a model of efficiency and profitability." TV, magazines, newspapers, the Internet — all could shed their parochial beginnings and join Ford, Chrysler, and General Motors and maybe even produce as many diverse products. With "modernization," one of the last of the silly old barriers — that between news reporting and advertising — also appears as an unnecessary vestige of the past. Welcome to postmodernity, boys and girls.

THE NEW JOURNALISM

A PR firm called Media Relations has been providing the following important advice for prospective business clients: "The media is separated into two categories. One is content and the other is advertising. They're both for sale." And what is the difference between the two? As MR explains, news stories are cheaper to place than advertisements. This "openness" to input on the part of news organizations is the result of financial pressures, contends MR. The days of reporters going out to find stories are over. Now they keep costs down by "relying on companies like ours to help them come up with story ideas and find sources." The PR firm goes on to add that for "many media outlets, we play such an active role helping them create stories that we're viewed as an extension of their production staff." It was not too many years ago that we actually needed radical critics like Ralph Nader or Noam Chomsky to expose the media's hidden closet. Now, all is proudly put on display.

EMPEROR'S CLOTHING DEPT.

In the pages of *Advertising Age*, advertising consultant Marian Salzman issued a timely warning to her colleagues. "Savvy consumers," she cautioned, "are increasingly aware of the cross-pollination between news and advertising." Gasp. I'm told many have also guessed the truth about Santa Claus. According to a poll Ms. Salzman cited, the public estimates that 48% of the news comes directly from handouts by corporations. The obviousness of this incestuous relationship led her to give the following warning: "Should the line between news and corporate PR or advertising efforts become too blurred, the public may object." The operative phrase here is "too blurred." Blurred is the assumed bottom line. We just don't want to be too greedy and leave Dan Rather, Barbara Walters, or *Newsweek* magazine without a fig leaf.

OBJECTIVE CHEERLEADING

Critics of the major TV networks, coverage of our bombing of Afghanistan had a number of favorite adjectives. Heading the list were "myopic," "superficial," "sugar-coated," and "knee-jerk pandering." So it was with some interest that I awaited a defense of the network's policy of sticking to Pentagon briefings instead of showing the civilian casualties the rest of the world was seeing. The honors went to Bill Wheatley, vice-president of NBC News, who presented a fine example of someone attempting a high jump, almost clearing the bar only to have the trailing knee knock it over. "[Our] coverage of the war isn't slanted in any way," he said. "We haven't shied away from dealing with the fact that there has been *collateral damage* ..." He couldn't say it. He couldn't get out of the Pentagon's framework and say "women and children killed" or "innocent civilian deaths." Just as an experiment, try referring to the victims of September 11th as "collateral damage."

Among those voicing appreciation for the role of the major TV networks from a slightly different perspective were a number of leaders in the advertising industry. *The Wall Street Journal* posed the following question to a panel of distinguished advertisers: "Should we try new national advertising in a time of crisis?" Among those who answered in the negative was Cheryl Berman, chief creative officer for Leo Burnett USA. "I wouldn't try it," she argued. "The news stations are already doing that for us." Duuh.

raising THe Bar

When 50,000 opponents of corporate globalization brought the meetings of the World Trade Organization to a halt in Seattle, all of the local TV stations except for the ABC affiliate, KOMO, provided live coverage of the "disturbances." KOMO-TV News Director Joe Barnes vowed that disruptive groups during the three-day WTO conference would not manipulate the station. While promising to cover WTO issues, Barnes said KOMO "will not devote coverage to irresponsible or illegal activities ..." The station returned to its important regular daytime programming of *All My Children, One Life to Live* and *General Hospital.* I'm told Mr. Barnes later explained the policy of not covering "irresponsible or illegal activities" would not be applied to car chases, crime scenes, or the environmental policies of the WTO.

CRAFT PRIDE RETURNS

Plans to present television's Emmy Awards to deserving commercials hit unexpected opposition. An industry group questioned whether or not advertisements actually qualify as TV programming. In a stunning setback, the New York-based National Academy of Television Arts and Sciences, which gives out the Emmys for daytime shows, ruled that "because advertising sells products, it doesn't qualify as programming." Behind the scenes, opposition was voiced in even stronger terms by critics who "can't stand to see the Emmys so debased." And just who was leading this fight to maintain the integrity of TV's highest honors? Who was the one group resisting the debasing inroads of commercialization? According to *The Wall Street Journal*, opposition was spearheaded by "the soap opera and game show crowd." Could they be our culture's last line of defense?

MUCKRAKING PRESS

Popular magazines have found a sure way to produce quality feature stories on Hollywood celebrities. Trusting the stars' obvious good judgment, they let them pick their own writers. *The Wall Street Journal* reported that magazines routinely let major stars veto questions, topics, and reporters who "look for the bad news," as *Good Housekeeping* editor Ellen Levine so delicately put it. Critics claim this results in celebrity puff pieces that are just cogs in the culture industry's marketing plans. But *Vanity Fair* editor Graydon Carter has a good retort: "You can only have so many tough things in an issue and I think it's foolish to waste it on an actor." We are still waiting to discover what constitutes a "tough thing" for *Vanity Fair*.

Many other familiar supermarket magazines have realized savings by simply eliminating reporters all together in their interviews of celebrities. Sharon Stone conducted her own interview in *Harper's Bazaar*, as did Mel Gibson in *Us*. While carping critics worry that such practices turn the press into extensions of Hollywood's PR machinery, Ingrid Sischy, editor of *Interview*, took a more positive view of "collaborating" with famous personalities: "We are taking people's portraits with these interviews and as you know, a portrait can be skewed in many ways." No reporter, no skewing. But even if a reporter is used, one imperative remains: "And if we feel any sense of discomfort about what we are doing ... I suggest we make a phone call." A courtesy politicians also appreciate.

Literary Pioneer

Novelist Fay Weldon may have helped drag literature into the 21st century with the publication of her novel *The Bulgari Connection*, a book described by marketing consultant Michael Nyman as "part of the next wave of product placement." The book was commissioned by the Italian jewelry company Bulgari and contains no less than 34 references to Bulgari jewelry. My personal favorite is this gem: "Lady Juliet's Bulgari necklace gleamed out, a source of power and influence." But not to be ignored is the erotic power of a simple phrasing such as "her Bulgari on my bosom."

Ms. Weldon has some fine advice for other authors who want to invite commercial sponsorship. Her first rule is "Let's do it honorably — without any pretense." The second rule is to go beyond mere name-dropping. "I can see where product placement is sleazy," she told reporters, "but I didn't product-place. I wrote a novel about a product, a good novel ..." (Note how quickly the verb *to product-place* has come into usage.) Many critics miss this fine distinction. Meanwhile, no less of an expert than futurist Faith Popcorn predicted that "many literary icons will look at this branding as a new art form, and it won't be considered sleazy at all." This will, of course, be counted as an advance in our sensibilities.

Writers Improve Their IQs

Years ago, culture critics commonly bemoaned the fate of authors whose novels became popular and were subsequently bought by Hollywood. They called it "selling out," I believe, because the studios would inevitably dilute and emasculate (or effeminate?) any original literary effort. But times have changed. With studios now offering millions to buy a book by authors like Michael Crichton and John Grisham, an important change has occurred. Warner

Brothers producer Denise Di Novi reported that a "lot of authors have gotten smart. [I knew it would happen someday.] They're laying out their books like movies; they're delivering what you need for a movie." That means a lot of short snappy scenes and roles for strong male leads. In fact, the smarter authors build their lead character with one of the half dozen top male stars in mind already (those being Tom Cruise, Harrison Ford, Tom Hanks, Mel Gibson and Brad Pitt). Now we needn't worry about independent authors selling out to Hollywood *after* they've written their novels.

CRUMBLING WALLS

Allure, a popular women's magazine, has been credited with taking an important step in overcoming the unfortunate legacy of the older practice of separating advertising and editorial content. The magazine, in what it called an "interactive editorial", praised makeup shades they say will look good on anyone. The editorial then became "interactive" by having samples of Revlon eye shadow and Johnson & Johnson Neutrogena blush (supplied by the manufacturer) glued to the same page. Linda Wells, *Allure*'s editor, defended this cooperation between editorial writers and advertisers in words that reveal the naiveté of critics. "We write about people who advertise in the magazine," she said. "That's what magazines do." It's so tiresome having to point out the obvious. Is it still necessary to give this kind of an explanation?

CUTTING-EDGE COMICS

A magazine for young men called *Details* found an even more startlingly unique way to involve its commercial sponsors. In one issue, *Details* featured a 24-page comic section that, according to *Advertising Age*, "weaves sponsors into the plot line of an edgy comic section". Not only did readers get to see their favorite ads from Mastercard, L'Oreal, Panasonic, and Sony, but they actually got to see their products used by cartoon characters just like real actors do in the movies. The comic book plot revolves around the adventures of a young in-line skater as he pursues the woman of his dreams while wearing his Lee jeans and splashing on some Hugo eau de toilette for good measure. *Advertising Age* described the exercise in erasing the boundaries between ads and magazine content as "breaking new ground." *Details* publisher Linda Mason went a step further. She described their ad/cartoon format as "synergistic." I always love it when publishers learn big words.

"SOMETIMES A GREAT NOTION"

Amazon.com was discovered to have been accepting payments from publishers of up to $10,000 to have books featured and reviewed on its website under the headings "Destined for Greatness" and "What We're Reading" (or what might be called "What We're Getting Paid To Tell You We're Reading"). Faced with public criticism for not disclosing the ongoing payments from publishers, Amazon found some resourceful responses. Vice-president Mary Morouse opposed labeling purchased reviews because of the often-overlooked "neatness" issue: "I think it would be more distracting to have a book tagged," she said. "I think that would clutter it up." Next at bat, Amazon founder Jeff Bezos argued his company was "pioneering a new medium that shouldn't be held up to the same standards" as book reviewers in magazines who strive for "independence from advertising concerns." After all, who can meet those high standards? Two years later Amazon spokesperson Kristin Schaeffer was heard defending the reduction of book recommendations to paid advertisements in these words: "Now we're allowing publishers to have input ..." More empowerment. But how do you make up for all those years in the wilderness when publishers were "denied" input?

HISTORY REWRITING 101

One of our culture's most common myths has finally been put to rest. Cynics complain that when large corporations buy out book publishers, the latter's work is inevitably compromised. Just the opposite was demonstrated by attorney Gary Reback at a conference on Microsoft sponsored by Ralph Nader. Earlier that year the software firm had bought out *Funk & Wagnall's Encyclopedia* to use for their on-line *Encarta* version. *Funk & Wagnall's* originally had an entry on none other than Bill Gates himself, describing him as a "tough competitor who seems to value winning in a competitive environment over money." A terrible sentence. After the takeover, this same phrase was improved to "known for his corporate contributions and educational organizations." Obviously a much better literary effort that leaves nothing compromised.

Have you forgotten who invented the telephone? If you look it up in most versions of the *Encarta Encyclopedia*, you would discover Alexander Graham Bell's name. But if you look it up in the Italian edition, you'd learn the inventor was Antonio Meucci. Similarly, in the American edition Thomas Edison and Britain's Joseph Swan "simultaneously" invented the light bulb, but in the British version Edison disappears. All of this was part of Microsoft's efforts to adapt its "products" to different markets. For example, Egypt's takeover of the Suez Canal in 1956 moved from being a "decisive" intervention of superpowers (U.S. edition) to a "humiliating reversal" to Britain and France in their editions. And Kurdistan disappears entirely in a Middle Eastern edition as *Encarta* fits facts to local sensibilities. But, as Bill Gates says, "exposing people to world-wide perspectives should be healthy." Except maybe for the poor "disappeared" people of Kurdistan.

TV FILLS THE VOID

Realizing a mere six hours a day of television viewing leaves many underutilized hours, TV networks have been reaching out to help give viewers something to do wherever they go. People in shopping mall food courts can watch the Cafe USA channel. At the bowling alley you can watch Strike 10 and then go to the video arcade for Channel M. Or if you decide to golf, you can catch Pinpoint Golf Advertising at our better courses. At the airport, the CNN Airport Network stands ready to meet your viewing needs, at your doctor's office it's the Better Health Network. There was even a children's network called Cartoon Cuts for those wasted

15-minutes spent getting a haircut. Better hotels, like Hilton's, installed TVs in their elevators because TV breaks up what they described as a socially "awkward situation." Answering critics' complaints of being forcibly bombarded by TV, John McMenamin, Turner Private Network's CEO, said, "We don't think of it as targeting captive audiences. We only want to do this where there is a meaningful fit between environment, audience, and the content of the programs." The next time you see a TV in a public space, you can point it out and exclaim, "Look, there's another 'meaningful fit'."

NeW, ImProveD PBS

The Public Broadcasting System has begun giving advertising executives the red carpet treatment at gala openings in New York and Los Angeles to promote their new fall shows. PBS unveiled what *The Wall Street Journal* described as its "new advertising savvy." With Federal funding cuts, PBS went out to attract corporate "underwriters" with promises of "fewer restrictions than before." PBS began allowing more shots of products and more extensive use of company slogans in their 15-second underwriter blurbs. In what could be the watchwords of the era, Senior VP Jonathan Abbot declared, "We have to do a more effective job at presenting ourselves to corporate decision-makers and funders." (Don't we all.) But not to worry that PBS might sacrifice hard-hitting documentaries in their rush to appease corporate executives, because PBS is restrained by its reputation. "Our brand," said Mr. Abbott, "is held by viewers in a high position of trust." Ah yes, right up there with Kellogg's Corn Flakes.

Concerns about public TV's commercialism were raised once again when Chicago's educational channel, WTTW, was fined by the Federal Communication Commission for airing improper or "enhanced" underwriter credits. The 30-second quasi-ads even raised concerns with the editorial writers at *Advertising Age*, who defended maintaining the legitimacy of public broadcasting: "Preserving distinctions between public TV and commercial TV is still important for public TV's future," the editors wrote, "both as an entertainment medium and as an advertising medium." At your local public station's next pledge drive, you might offer praise for their newly recognized status as a commercial vehicle.

Nature aBHOrs a vacuum

Video production engineers finally solved a problem that had plagued the broadcasting of old reruns on TV. Classic shows like *I Love Lucy, Gilligan's Island* and *All in the Family* were produced before advertisers had mastered the art of product placement. This meant that valuable film footage on TV was being commercially wasted. Now engineers for companies like Princeton Video and DeWitt Media can insert brand name beer cans and potato chip packages into old shows and even give them the look of the original production. This exciting advance has raised concerns about a possible backlash by consumers to obvious commercials wandering into the programs. That's why Gene DeWitt, chairman of DeWitt Media, adds a cautionary note: "I'm big on exploitation," he says (Aren't we all?), "but not to the point where it is self-defeating." Maybe someday, in a better world, we'll be ready for the real thing.

Princeton Video Image then went one step further. If you've ever been to a baseball game, you may have noticed empty spaces with no advertising. Well, help has arrived, at least for TV viewers, thanks to Princeton's ability to insert virtual billboards onto the TV screen. Programmers can literally add a Coke ad to the low wall behind a Ken Griffey Jr. while he's batting. The virtual ads, which have been used at soccer and wrestling events, look quite real because the computer even compensates as the camera zooms in or out. According to *The Wall Street Journal*, virtual ads offer "a way to hold viewers' attention during key plays, rather than waiting for commercial breaks." In short, there's no wasted time. Fortunately, the networks still recognize, according to ESPN's Bob Jeremiah, that "the commercials shouldn't compete with the event." It's hard, but sometimes you do need to exercise self-restraint.

Now that the technology for virtual ads is in place, we are certainly going to need standards for when and how many new product placements are appropriate for, say, a rerun of *Gilligan's*

Island. Paul Slagle, a marketing VP with Princeton Video, came up with a good rule of thumb. "It's only a bad idea," he says, "if you do it in a nonorganic way." You want to make sure the product placement (or, as some prefer to call it, the "product integration") doesn't "take away from the creative process." Of course, if there is no creative process or "organic" plot to detract from, I presume it's open season.

SPONSOr-FrieNDLY TV PrograMS

Advertisers worry that many people are not watching their ads on TV and so have turned to product placement. Warren Weideman of Park Avenue Productions said that "product placement is a way to combat the threat of consumers not watching commercials." Because of the way many of us have been falling down on the job, corporations like Pepsi, Coca-Cola, McDonald's, and Annhauser-Busch now have to spend millions to have their products written into the scripts of trend-setting programs like CBS's *Survivor*. Coke, for example, will be paying $6 million for ad placements on the *Young Americans* program. But this will be no abrupt or crude intrusion into the plot. Coke's spokesperson Jeff Dunn emphasized, "We want to be integrated naturally into *Young Americans*." The concern for artistic integrity lives on.

Those who'd like to get a glimpse of the direction TV programming may take need to look south to *Sabado Gigante*, South and North America's most popular Spanish-language variety show. This four-hour Saturday night entertainment spectacle found a way to dramatically cut production costs — by simply letting its advertisers write the show, thus cutting out unnecessary middlemen. The producers of this trend-setting "product placement fantasy," as *The Wall Street Journal* described it, not only met regularly with sponsors to come up with scripts, but also gave them final approval (just like Congress). Such friendly treatment drew in major corporations like McDonald's, Sears, Mars Inc., and AT&T. During the show, host Mario Kreutzberger not only led the audience in sing-alongs to advertising jingles but also participated in corporate-written skits about their products, featuring scantily clad female models. Said Steve Farley, a VP at Payless Drugs, "They have woven us into the program seamlessly, and the people love it."

DeFeNDING THe CONSTITUTION

Television broadcasters have worked hard to pull off a skillful doubleplay. First, they marshaled legions of lobbyists to convince the Federal Communications Commission to grant them new free broadcast frequencies for digital TV, an estimated $20- to $50-billion bargain. Descriptions of this ranged from *The Wall Street Journal*'s "giveaway to broadcasters" to Sen. John McCain's "one of the greatest scams in American history." But once granted a new chunk of public airwaves, the companies had to hold off pressures to act "in the public interest" (as the law requires) by providing up to an entire half-hour of free air time to Congressional candidates. Easy. That requirement was, said the National Association of Broadcasters, clearly "an infringement of their first amendment rights," which includes the well-known right not to let others speak. Imagine how the Founding Fathers would have protested if they had known a half hour of Jerry Springer or America's Funniest Home Videos might be canceled for a mere political speech. In the words of A. J. Liebling, "Freedom of the press belongs to those who own one."

MOVIe UPGraDeS

NBC made some last minute improvements to its suspense movie *Atomic Train*. The movie was originally about a train going out of control while carrying a nuclear bomb and nuclear waste. After heavily promoting the movie's factual basis, NBC suddenly changed its mind with "no input" from its parent company, General Electric, who — this really isn't very important — just happens to be a big investor in nuclear power. Alerted to the "fact" that nuclear wastes are not transported by trains, they added a disclaimer emphasizing the movie's fictional character, which they showed at every commercial break. Then NBC replaced every mention of nuclear waste with the phrase "hazardous waste," thereby achieving that prized look of a dubbed Japanese horror film. Meanwhile there was a bill before Congress to allow the shipping by rail of 77,000 tons of nuclear waste (make that "hazardous waste") through 43 states. I was going to check to see if they rewrote the objectionable phrase properly but then I decided to go to the beach instead. Sometimes you just need to trust your elected representatives.

MONOPOLY BENEFITS US ALL

Since the 1996 Telecommunications Act relaxed ownership rules for radio, large corporations like Westinghouse, CBS, and Chancellor Media have been gobbling up stations at a record rate. The Big Three now run half of the radio ads in the top six markets. By buying up stations nationwide, radio chains can offer their advertisers a site for "one stop shopping," a tremendous advantage that is one of two factors luring large corporations to radio advertising. The other is traffic congestion. Big traffic jams and long commutes allow advertisers to reach more people by radio. Lynn Greiner, media manager for Penney's, said, "Now we are able to reach women as they are driving to work or taking their kids to soccer practice." This prospect makes advertisers gleeful. Scott Ginsburg, CEO of Cancellor Media, said, "While other people stuck in traffic get very frustrated and angry, I tend to giggle." Just remember those words during your next traffic jam. You're helping an important executive feel very happy.

Helpful Hints

Those who'd like to expand their appreciation of the media may want to study the artistic means developed by the legendary Joey Skaggs: the hoax. Among my favorites is the story of how Skaggs sold ABC on a story of a Cathouse for Dogs with "actual" video footage of the canine brothel. Or the Celebrity Sperm Bank the press "exposed" that came complete with "protesters." Both required the teamwork of many aspiring actresses and actors, an

added benefit. Skaggs explains a key advantage of his culture jamming in terms that bear repeating: "I can't call a press conference
to talk about how the media has been turned into a government
propaganda machine, manipulating us into believing we've got to
go to war in the Middle East. But as a jammer, I can go into these
issues in the process of revealing a hoax."

For those who'd prefer something on a smaller scale, there is
always television recycling. This makes a wonderful public cere-
mony and is said to bring good luck. I recommend using at least
a ten-pound sledge hammer. You may want to cover the set with
a sheet or towel so that broken glass does not fly off and cut anyone. Be sure to take turns.

Postmodern Censorship

C ENSORSHIP USED TO be such a straightforwardly crude affair, with these wrinkly old crones waving their umbrellas and shrilly demanding an end to rampant immorality. Those were the good old days, when Doris Day always wore snappy pajamas and slept safely away from her "husband" in the security of a double bed. Now that we are all hip, censorship has, with notable exceptions, moved on. In the culture of narcissism, our concern is not about strange, repressed sexual passions, but about ensuring that the party goes on without any unpleasant reminders of the poverty or suffering of those left outside in the rain. An even deeper concern of ours is making sure that our finer commercial products appear in appropriate environments. Let us begin our tour.

ADVANCED NUMBING

Clear Channel Communications, owners of 1,200 radio stations nationwide, responded to the September 11th tragedy by "graylisting" 150 songs they labeled "lyrically questionable." In what management described as a "grass-roots movement," the nation's largest radio chain suggested to disc jockeys they not play songs that failed to "support a high level of patriotism."

From that list, here is my list of the Top Ten worst offenders:
1. "Imagine" by John Lennon,
2. "Peace Train" by Cat Stevens,
3. Louis Armstrong's "What a Wonderful World,"
4. "Bridge Over Troubled Water" by Simon and Garfunkel,
5. Neil Diamond's "America,"
6. "Ticket to Ride" by the Beatles,
7. "On Broadway" by The Drifters,
8. "American Pie" by Don McLean,
9. "Get Together" by The Youngbloods,
10. All songs by Rage Against the Machine.

This puts us in the *Guinness Book of World Records* as the world's first society ever to conceive of the possibility of censoring Neil Diamond.

SPreaDING THe VIrus

A dozen American high-tech companies jumped in to bid for the opportunity to help a struggling developing country. The royal government of Saudi Arabia has seen the need to assist its country's half a million Internet users make the best choices as they surf the Net and has turned to the West for software that will block inappropriate Web sites. "The Internet is a frightening place to some people," said Matthew Holt, the overseer of sales operations for Secure Computing. "The government feels the need to intervene." (Rumor has it Secure Computing has also offered to tuck in users at night.)

Since all Internet traffic to Saudi Arabia is funneled through a single center near Riyadh, the Saudi Arabian government has a wonderful opportunity to protect its citizens not only from pornography, but also from unwanted political sites promoting human and political rights. Should American companies be actively supporting such censorship? Secure Computing's Mr. Holt makes an important point: "Once we sell them the product," he said, "we can't enforce how they use it." An excellent point, one usually appreciated only by the more refined of cigarette and semi-automatic rifle manufacturers.

ACTIVIST PLAYGROUNDS

Ever since the WTO demonstrations in Seattle, planners for large public events have had to deal with the problem of how to balance the rights of protesters and those of visitors. The Winter Olympics in Utah announced a fine solution, providing five small "parks" for protest groups to use. The "protest zones" would allow from ten to a hundred protesters to exercise their free speech rights. Groups interested in demonstrating just need to sign up for a time slot and obtain a permit. Scott Folsom, the Salt Lake City Police's chief Olympic planner, put it succinctly: "What we're trying to do is establish areas where we know it can be managed." He did not say if slides and swings would be provided for the protesters.

Have you ever wondered why you so rarely hear about protesters at campaign appearances by presidential candidates? Or even critical questions being asked? It's the result of what Ginny Terzano, Al Gore's former press secretary, describes as "Advance Work 101". In these highly choreographed appearances, protesters are kept at a distance by a simple expedient: tickets. You have to have a ticket issued by the local party to get close to the candidates. But to ensure the rights of protesters, organizers provide them with their own roped-off "protest area" (sort of like child playrooms at some theatres). Sometimes these areas are only about the length of a football field removed from the podium. Whether binoculars are provided for the protesters is not clear ... And pesky reporters? Ms. Terzano openly says the decision of whether to grant interviews is "based on whether the campaign thinks a favorable story will result." Only in America can we be so open and frank.

BUY NOTHING DAY

A rather subversive organization called Adbusters, out of Vancouver, Canada, has gained notoriety for producing parodies and anti-advertisements. One of their finer efforts has repeatedly failed to meet the high standards of our major networks. Set against the backdrop of a pig, the ad questions over-consumption, calling on consumers to participate in Buy Nothing Day, scheduled for the day after Thanksgiving. Despite Adbusters' coming with cash in their hands, the ad was rejected by NBC because, in the words of VP Richard Gitter, the ad was "inimical to our legitimate business interests." An understandable reply. But CBS went the extra mile. First they stated they couldn't run the ad because it was an "advocacy ad," as if ads for General Motors or Nike weren't advocating anything. (What an insult to their agencies.) Then they presented their killer argument. They announced they had to reject the ad because Buy Nothing Day was "in opposition to the current economic policy in the United States." You might want to write CBS and find out what criminal penalties can be invoked against non-consumers.

TOO MaNY BIG WOrDS

The ACLU filed a lawsuit after a school district in Anaheim, California, removed ten books from the shelves of Orangeview Junior High School. The books were a series of biographies of important gays and lesbians, such as James Baldwin, Oscar Wilde, Marlene Dietrich, Liberace, John Maynard Keynes, and Martina Navratilova. But you may all breathe a sigh of relief: it turned out the books were not removed because of their homosexual content. Instead, said school district officials, they were removed because the reading level was "too high" for their students. In addition, they worried that children might be harassed if seen reading such books (not, I believe, because of the high reading level but because of the content). Since the library is obviously short of books now, you can help by sending books that match the district's expectations for junior high readers. May I suggest Dr. Seuss?

"JUST SaY NO" DePT.

Those who remember the horrors of marijuana smoking portrayed in the classic film *Reefer Madness* will want to obtain copies of a pamphlet entitled *How Parents Can Help Children Live Marijuana Free*. Upstanding Senators like Orrin Hatch (R-Utah) were actively promoting this pamphlet. Besides providing valuable information on the dangers of drug usage, this leaflet broke new ground in recognizing some of the signs of pot smoking. These include "excessive preoccupation with social causes, race relations, environmental issues, etc." Finally, we have both an explanation for why people get wrapped up in political movements and the means to ferret out these devious pot addicts. It's too bad we can't just train dogs to sniff out individuals carrying liberal and environmental books and then cart them off to drug rehabilitation centers.

"FIrST THeY came FOr THe COMMUNISTS, aND I DIDN'T SPeak UP ..."

In a decision that shocked lovers of great literature, the Villanova University Bookstore announced it would no longer carry Cliff's Notes. These handy abridgements of the classics have saved two generations of students from wading through the actual texts. Cliff's Notes took out a full-page ad in the school newspaper to accuse the University of censorship, arguing the ban was "an affront to the diverse student population that university officials claim to support." They did not elaborate on exactly why it was an affront to "diversity." But coming to Cliff's defense was Professor Richard Wolffson of Montclair State University. Noting that students who don't want to read can get their Cliff's Notes fix anywhere, he argued teachers had to take leadership. "It's their responsibility," he said, "to add deeper meaning than even the notes can provide ..." Deeper meaning than Cliff's Notes!? Are we ready for this step? Meanwhile, defenders of civil liberties for jocks were asking, "If they can ban Cliff's Notes, what's next?" Classic Comics? Readers Digest? Tom Brokaw?

STUDeNT CeNSOrSHIP MaDe SIMPLe

In this day and age, it's sometimes a challenge for school administrators to come up with convincing rationales for exercising control over student publications. Fortunately, some brave souls have been mapping out fresh terrain, like principal Tom Paulsen of Naperville Central High in Illinois. Faced with student reporters who had unearthed evidence of administrators overspending on travel during a budget crisis, Paulsen did the only thing possible. He censored the students' news story. His reason? "My concern," he said, "was that there may have been an appearance that these administrators did something wrong, and that would affect their ability to lead." An appearance of wrong? Tsk, tsk. But remember, according to the Supreme Court's famous *Hazelwood* decision, principals can censor material that interferes with a school's "basic educational mission." Certainly, hordes of embarrassed administrators would clearly undermine any basic educational mission.

LaNGUaGe CLeaNSerS

For the past 20 years, *Merriam-Webster's Collegiate Thesaurus* has listed a large number of interesting synonyms for the word *homosexual*. Included were such common terms as *faggot, fruit, uranist, nancy,* and the ever popular *pederast*. This "corporate mistake," as *The New York Times* described it, was finally corrected in their new edition. To ensure a more sensitive approach to gays, Merriam-Webster resorted to a simple expedient. They just eliminated *homosexual* from the thesaurus. The demotion of *homosexual* to an un-word (as we say in Newspeak) was defended by marketing director Deborah Burns citing a sudden discovery that thesauruses, unlike dictionaries, need not be comprehensive (try that as an advertising slogan) and explaining that entries for ethnic and racial minorities had already been removed. Hopefully this move will help remove prejudice against homosexuals because, of course, we won't have the words for it any more.

MISS MaNNerS' "DeFeNDerS OF NOrMaLCY"

When Atlanta tidied up its streets for guests at the Olympics, Anita Beatry of the Atlanta Task Force on the Homeless revealed that 9,000 arrests of homeless persons had been made in the preceding 12 months, four times more than the previous Atlanta record. City officials were assisted by a tough ordinance destined for Newspeak fame. The law allows police to arrest people for "acting in a manner not usual for law-abiding individuals" in parking lots and garages. Those who had been determined to be acting "not usual" could be sentenced to up to six months in jail or to a public works project. You have to admire the leaders of Atlanta for knowing what was "usual" behavior for us law-abiding folks (notice how quickly I jumped in to join this group).

Citizens in Salida City, Colorado, in an effort to wipe out the scourge of "loitering," passed a bill that would prohibit adults from spending more than five minutes in a public place after 11 p.m. The ordinance outlawed the disgraceful practice of people staying too long in one location, which it defined as "any two points within two hundred feet of each other." Despite trivial objections that this makes waiting in lines at theaters illegal, supporters have stuck to their position following a few initial compromises. The original bill, for example, not only prohibited "loitering," but also "lingering," "tarrying" (my personal favorite), or "standing idly about." And it wasn't limited to just after 11 p.m. but covered the day as well. Unfortunately, the language about "standing idly about," I'm told, proved to be too descriptive of the city council that enacted the ordinance and had to be dropped.

My personal favorite amongst efforts to support appropriate behavior is the rules approved by the exclusive community of Coral Gables in Florida. Their city commission has outlawed "impertinence." Let me quote to you from the regulation: "Any person making impertinent or slanderous remarks or who becomes boisterous while addressing the commission shall be barred from further audience." (Sounds like cruel and unusual punishment.) Clapping was also outlawed. Lest you think this was a fluke, Coral Gables has also banned the parking of pickup trucks in front of houses.

aDVerTISers BecoMe LITeraTe

Major advertisers have been "changing the rules of magazine publishing," reported *The Wall Street Journal*, by breaking down the walls separating ads from editorial content. A number of corporations began demanding written summaries of articles before submitting their ads. Chrysler sent out a letter to *Esquire* and 100 other magazines informing them that in "an effort to avoid potential conflicts, it is required that Chrysler Corporation be alerted in advance of any and all editorial content that encompasses sexual, political, social issues or any editorial content that could be construed as provocative or offensive." I particularly like that "could be construed" part. Really professional. Countering critics who worried about freedom of the press, Pentacom CEO David Martin pointed out the reasonableness of advertisers' demands because, given that ads cost $22,000 a piece, "you want it surrounded by positive things." (Happy thoughts, I believe he meant). *Esquire* certainly agreed. After receiving their letter from Chrysler, they canceled a scheduled story with a gay theme by author David Leavitt. Probably not positive enough.

When it was discovered that Chrysler was demanding pre-notification from magazine editors, a small furor erupted. Faced with protests from publishers, Chrysler apparently backed down — apparently. Chrysler spokesman Michael Aberlich announced, "We don't want notifications. We won't read them." (Rumor had it that three executives were hired to "not read" any notifications.) Mr. Aberlich also announced Chrysler would handle the problem by just becoming "a lot more conservative in picking magazines for its ads." But what should publishers do with articles that may offend the sensitivities of Chrysler? Simple. Mr. Aberlich tells them, "You know our guidelines. We're sure you will use good judgment." But at least Chrysler won't be censoring the content.

Despite Chrysler's best efforts, they finished second to Coca-Cola in the new field of providing guidance for magazine publishers. Christine Maggiore, print media buyer for McCann-Erickson, Coca-Cola's major advertising agency, sent a memo to publishers advising them that they "believe that positive and upbeat editorial provides a compatible environment in which to communicate the brand's message." Ever willing to be helpful, she then went on to list the subjects Coca-Cola considered to be "inappropriate." As expected, articles discussing politics, environmental issues, "sex related issues," and drugs headed the list. But there were also some surprising categories to be axed. Not only did articles on health and food fail the test, but also the whole category of hard news took a dive — not happy enough. We are still searching for whatever categories may be left.

Happy Spaces

In an effort to keep pace with the times, the Leo Burnett Ad Agency distributed a 30-page internal memo recommending that its top client, McDonald's, avoid advertising on shows with homosexual content. The memo suggested setting "parameters so that McDonald's continues to appear in a suitable environment." Fitting into the most suitable environment has meant McDonald's has "traditionally avoided homosexual content when possible" because it's a "hot topic" for their Bible belt franchise operators. Unfortunately, the memo warned, gay characters "are becoming more difficult to avoid." Isn't that so true? Meanwhile, following criticism from the Gay and Lesbian Alliance Against Defamation, another ad executive, David McQuaid, defended the Leo Burnett agency in the pages of *Advertising Age*. "It would seem natural," McQuaid argued, "for an agency to pick the best environment possible for its client's ads." Absolutely. If only gays and lesbians could work just a bit harder at being nice they too could be a positive space for Big Macs.

Quality Control

Literary interest has been flowering among the executives of our nation's major chain stores. Big discount centers like Winn-Dixie and Wal-Mart were following Chrysler's example and demanded advance copies of magazines carried by their stores. Not only do they get the pleasure of reading articles first, they can also protect their customers from unwanted material. For example, the Winn-Dixie chain banned an issue of *Cosmopolitan* for a headline about "His and Her Orgasms." Winn-Dixie regularly bans not only questionable photos, but also articles on topics like abortion, homosexuality, and religion. Said spokesperson G.E. Clerc Jr., "We would prefer that their publications didn't offend anyone." Fortunately, as *The Wall Street Journal* reported, "Publishers are increasingly anticipating retail chains' concerns." Even so, Wal-Mart manager Teresa Stanton reported, "every other week I pull something off the shelf that I don't think is of Wal-Mart quality." Publishers have proven to be surprisingly slow at grasping such higher-order concepts as "Wal-Mart quality."

Meanwhile, Wal-Mart's crusade to clean up song lyrics for our nation's youth gained a boost when C. Delores Tucker and Mr. Virtue himself, William J. Bennett, penned an op-ed in their support. Answering critics' charges that Wal-Mart was stifling freedom of speech, the two declared, "It is absurd to call this censorship." What then are we to call the practice of "re-editing" and "sanitizing" songs and refusing to sell objectionable CDs? In their words, "Wal-Mart is exercising quality control — which it does every day for every product." Thus an offensive Boys2Men rap song is to be treated like a mangled can of Drano. Now that we have moved on to "quality control," we need not bother ourselves with quaint concepts like "censorship." It's untidy to have unemployed words lying about. Let's just hope the "quality control" engineers at Wal-Mart get to wear those nifty little white coats. They look so professional.

QUEEN VICTORIA'S REVENGE

A trailblazing ordinance was presented to the city council in Laramie, Wyoming, that would expand the definition of the "nudity" to be banned in public places. All right-thinking people who have ever had to view the posterior of a certain type of beer-bellied construction worker will applaud the first part of the proposed law. It would have prohibited showing the cleft of the buttocks. But the next section of the original law is a truly important advance that covers a part of the male body that may be clothed yet "exposed" at the same time. The ordinance expanded the definition of nudity to include covered "male genitals in a discernibly turgid state." The law did not spell out the duties of police officers, but we're sure Laramie's finest would have been vigilant in seeking out erect or "discernibly turgid" genitals on males. I can just see officers asking "suspects" Mae West's famous question, "Sir, is that a pistol in your pocket or are you just glad to see me?"

HOMOSEXUAL WATCH

The Navy employed a piece of detective work worthy of Sherlock Holmes to unmask a homosexual within their midst. A veteran submarine officer with the unfortunate name of Timothy R. McVeigh (not related) was tracked down from information provided on his American Online Internet account. Although his dismissal from the Navy was blocked by a Federal judge, the Navy wins plaudits for the impeccable reasoning they employed to determine from his answer of "gay" to a questionnaire that he was a practicing homosexual. The following are the words of an actual yet unnamed Navy official: "Under the Department of Defense homosexuality conduct practice, the statement made by a member that he is gay provides the refutable presumption that the service member has a propensity to engage in homosexual conduct." And presumably heterosexuals have a similar "propensity" to engage in heterosexual conduct? In which case the entire Roman Catholic priesthood should do what?

Helpful Hints

Even when you disagree with someone's views, it is important to be helpful. For example, when the first Walk for Capitalism occurred in Seattle to celebrate globalism and free trade, anti-WTO groups decided that in place of the usual counter-demonstration, they'd help the pro-capitalism marchers "clarify " their message. So they dressed up in what the news media described as "capitalism chic," wearing suits, ties, and argyle sweater vests and having their hair carefully slicked back and evenly parted. The born-again "capitalists" led chants of "Shop, shop, shop" and carried signs that read, "Capitalism is Better than Democracy" and "Child Labor is Best for America: Smaller Hands Mean Tighter Stitches." The media, of course, ate it up, giving the two dozen "corporate helpers" the kind of friendly coverage that 2,000 traditionally strident protesters never could have attained.

Department of Down-sizing

AFTER A QUANTUM LEAP like the discovery of the term *down-sizing* to describe employee firings, it's hard to believe there was any room for advances in this field. Where do you go? But time marches on and now even *downsizing* is passé in the corporate-employee bonding lingo. The top honors for the advance go, as far as I know, to Wang Global for their discovery of *rightsizing*. When Wang announced their purchase of a firm named Olsy from Olivetti S.p.A., Wang predicted they would spend over $380 million on the "integration and the rightsizing of the new combined company." Notice the ease and dexterity with which the freshly minted verb *to rightsize* was employed. It reflects the new era of sensitivity to personal relationships that marks the way corporations relate to their employees today. After I'm through vomiting at that last sentence, I plan to sit and wait patiently for the first American company to introduce the term *nicesizing*, while you peruse these fine samples of corporate Newspeak.

rightsizing the english language

AT&T's official 150-page downsizing manual leaked out — and just in time for those of you who still speak of employees being fired or even laid off. No more. When AT&T fired 40,000 workers (as we would say in Oldspeak), they were really just carrying out a "force management program" aimed at reducing an "imbalance of forces and skills." Got it. Let's go on. Employees not invited back are simply labeled "unassigned," and a dismissal notice is an "involuntary offer" to work elsewhere. Even though AT&T speaks proudly of maintaining a loyal corporate family, human resources VP James Meadows warned that "people need to look upon themselves as vendors who come to this company to sell their skills." Jobs, he said, are being replaced by "projects" and workers need to see themselves as "contingent." So much for family values. Welcome to the age of the disposable Kleenex. However, not to despair: at least in two departments, old-fashioned loyalty still matters. While 40,000 jobs had been "unassigned," none were in PR or human resources.

hip redneck sheriff revival

Nike had to engage in major damage control because of charges that paying people 40 cents an hour to make shoes is exploitative. In Indonesia, many of the 100,000 Nike employees had been engaged in impromptu strikes. Nike spokesman Tony Nava set the tone early by assuring reporters that Nike backed the government's crackdown on independent unions and "illegal strikes." In the last strike, Nava reported, six "guys" were arrested but then released. "A few were fired," he said in a fine model of PR spin, but they were "the real troublemakers." Obviously, just the fact that all of Nike's Indonesian workers combined made less than spokesperson Michael Jordan was no reason for discontent. But there always have to be a few "real troublemakers" to wreck the party. This poses the question of just which 1930s Steinbeck novel Nike was recycling its script from? It's refreshing to see a company with a hip image retaining its ties to tradition, in this case the Southern tradition of hospitality to "outside agitators."

Later, none less than *The Wall Street Journal* came to Nike's defense. "Actually," lectured the *Journal*, "Nike Inc. says the hourly wage is about 42 cents which is twice Indonesia's legal minimum." Before praising Nike for their over-generosity, we might want to ask one small question: How was this minimum wage calculated? If the editors had bothered to look at the pages of *The New York Times*, they would have noticed Marzuki Usman, chair of the Jakarta Stock Exchange, explaining that the "philosophy of the minimum wage is to make sure the minimum calorie need per day is fulfilled." That's hopefully about 2,000 calories a day, although that figure was once a hot topic of debate in German concentration camp circles. Nike was paying twice that figure, which should allow for clothing and maybe even housing. But Nike was willing to pay twice the minimum despite fears, voiced by spokesperson Jim Small, that "Indonesia could be reaching a point where it is pricing itself out of the market." Thank God altruism is still alive and well.

reTurn OF THe UGLY american

Two lawsuits were filed in United States federal courts on behalf of 50,000 garment workers in the U.S.-protected Commonwealth of the Northern Mariana Islands. The suits charge U.S. retailers with engaging in a "racketeering conspiracy" to force workers largely from mainland China to accept intolerable sweatshop conditions. Named in the suits were firms such as The Gap, Tommy Hilfiger, Sears, Wal-Mart, and Oshkosh B'gosh. But one corporation in this group stood above the rest because of the effort they've made to defend workers' rights. The Gap went the extra mile, placing a poster in all the factories it subcontracted work to, with a clearly worded "code of conduct," written in proper English, itemizing the rights of employees. It certainly was not The Gap's fault that the Chinese workers did not know how to read English. How was The Gap to know that their Chinese workers only read Chinese? I say it serves them right. Those workers can just damn well learn to read English.

early warning signs

The Borders bookstore chain found itself inconvenienced by union activity. As a result, Anne Kubek of its Human Resources Dept. prepared a manual on "Union Awareness Training for Borders Managers." Someone was kind enough to post the whole text on the Internet — as a public service. Of particular value is a section entitled "Recognizing the Early Signs of Union Activity," a concern I know we all share. Here are a few of the warning signals with appropriate commentary:

1. "Employees gather in small groups of twos and threes and immediately halt their conversations when managers approach." (Could be bad breath.)
2. "Employees start gathering to talk in areas that are off the beaten path." (Obvious sign of nonconformity.)
3. "Employees who are not normally seen talking to one another begin associating more regularly. Strange alliances begin to form." (Sounds eerie. Notify the writers of the *X-files.*)
4. "New vocabulary may creep into employees' conversations. Union terms such as seniority, grievance, bumping, job security, job posting, etc. may appear in conversations." (Employees could be part of a *Reader's Digest* "Increase Your Word Skills" Club.)
5. "Managers start getting an inordinate amount of critical and probing questions concerning policies and/or benefits." (Employees might be awake on the job. Try diluting the coffee.)

So keep vigilant. You never know where the virus of Thoughtcrime will strike next.

"getting to know you"

Microsoft received substantial criticism for exploiting temporary workers by hiring them for what really were long-term positions and then keeping them on for years at the lower temp wages. Recognizing the problem, Microsoft announced a new policy:

temporary employees would just be required to leave their jobs for a month after a year's employment. Was this just a way to skirt around Washington State labor laws? No. Microsoft has an even loftier goal. Sharon Decker, director of contingent staffing, stated that the "change is intended to strengthen temps' relationships with the employment agencies that are their employers of record." Temps everywhere were heard sighing in relief as finally someone had recognized their primal need to bond with their payroll (or "moneylaundering") agencies.

NeW-aGe LaBor reLaTIONS

How does a hip Seattle latte company view employees who protest working conditions? Starbucks courageously faced an "unstrike" by employees in the Canadian province of British Columbia. Unionized workers continued on the job and handed out leaflets to customers and even wore union buttons. Senior VP Wanda Herndon said, "It is very disappointing that we have a fraction of our partners who want to have a third party that would come between our relationship." The "partners," as Starbucks calls its employees, earn the minimum wage in British Columbia, $5.15 an hour in U.S. currency. The shameless homewrecker was the Canadian Auto Workers, who now organize service workers and have even threatened Starbucks with a strike. In words that reportedly caused Henry Ford to roll over in his grave, Ms. Herndon responded, "[Starbucks Chairman] Howard Schultz is heartbroken that this has occurred because we have a really wonderful and unique relationship with our partners." Howard, we all feel for you and are with you in your pain, but do get a life!

NeW ParaDIGMS

General Motors generated some world-class Newspeak when answering charges that, according to their own figures, they have been cutting back on investments in the United States while building new plants in Argentina, Brazil, Poland, and China. GM spokesman Gerald Holmes rose to the occasion by explaining how misleading those figures were. Why? "The level of investment is not important," he argued, "because GM has been working to make its investments more efficient ... It's not indicative that we're doing less we're doing more with less." Upon hearing this, union officials were heard uttering a collective "Du-uh, why didn't we think of that?" I'm told that one lone cynic was overheard suggesting that GM executives might want to set an example by "doing more with less" compensation. That's why I never invite cynics over to my house.

GREAT SUCKING SOUND REVISITED

Sometimes it helps to cast fresh light on old problems. For example, when the North American Free Trade Agreement was implemented, critics predicted that greedy U.S. corporations would shut down their U.S. plants and reopen them in Mexico. But thanks to a report by John Sweeney of the right-wing Heritage Foundation, we can now see the situation in its proper perspective. It turns out that our automobile makers have not been fleeing the country. Instead, says Sweeney, the "automotive industry — one of the most important sectors of Michigan's economy — has engaged in greater cross-border, intra-industry specialization since NAFTA went into effect." Now isn't that a more positive way to describe corporate flight? Mexico specializes in production, while we specialize in ... what was it again?

HONOR AMONG THIEVES DEPT.

Major corporations have found a new way to avoid costly trials and convictions for breaking the law. *The Wall Street Journal* reported that "corporations under government investigation are increasingly turning on their employees to win leniency for themselves." This has proven to be a win-win solution (except for the employees left holding the bag) thanks to the 1991 U.S. Sentencing Guidelines that grant leniency to companies who apply "adequate discipline" to their employees. For example, when Darling International was accused of illegally dumping blood in the Blue Earth River in Minnesota, instead of stonewalling, Darling immediately found four employees to blame and even provided incriminating evidence to the government. Federal prosecutors such as Craig Benedict like this because "you get a lot more justice a lot more quickly." One reason is that corporations can force employees to answer questions because they can threaten to fire them, an incentive the government currently lacks. See what benefits cooperation can bring?

WISDOM OF MOBIL OIL

In an enlightening series of ads appearing in leading newspapers, Mobil Oil spelled out what countries must do to remain competitive in the world market. Citing the World Economics Forum's new "Competitiveness Index," Mobil listed such elements as "openness" to foreign investment and "labor market flexibility." (The later term, I'm told, refers to how far workers are willing to bend over for employers.) And what country, you ask, leads the world in competitiveness? Mobil proudly puts at the top of the list that well-known human rights "leader" Singapore, famed for caning visiting British tourists. Congratulations are also due to the United States, which placed third behind Hong Kong. Singapore and countries like Indonesia (15th) benefited from the fact that, according to *The New York Times*, "human rights appear to have no direct impact on competitiveness." The most "disappointing group" in the survey were European nations which "all provide high living standards" that interfere with the "efficiencies" of the market. Two nations — the Netherlands (12th) and Ireland (16th) — improved their ratings significantly by, in the *Times'* words, "making their welfare states more user-friendly for business." And what are Mobil and other U.S. corporations doing to help struggling Third World countries? Just listen to Mobil's ad: "American multinationals ... carry with us, for example, a standard of business ethics that provides a strong example of good ways to conduct business." Ah yes, the White Man's Burden never ends.

FROM BEHIND THE CURTAIN

Enron, Texas' favorite natural gas and electricity company, made many important contributions before its untimely demise. Certainly the publication of *The Enron Code of Ethics* helped advance the standards of corporate responsibility. Enron also made less known advances in the field of employee relations. Their website once proudly proclaimed that the "success of Enron lies not only in our products but also within each member of our team." A slight correction of this philosophy emerged when Enron CEO Jeffrey Skilling addressed an industry conference in Arizona. Behind closed doors, Mr. Skilling told fellow executives that job cuts in their industry were inevitable. "You must cut costs ruthlessly by 50 or 60 percent," he said. "Depopulate. Get rid of people. They gum up the works." Valued team members gumming up the works? This leak is reminiscent of the scene in *The Wizard of Oz* when the curtain is pulled to reveal the small man behind the PR image of the Wizard. They might want to keep those curtains closed a bit tighter.

Leadership in Fighting Sweatshops

The Eddie Bauer Co. was honored by the U.S. Department of Labor for their efforts to combat poor working conditions for garment workers. The sportswear chain is now one of 34 companies on the government's "Trendsetter List" of companies battling sweatshop conditions. But somehow left unmentioned by the Labor Department and the media was one small piece of information on just how Eddie Bauer is able to use American labor and still remain competitive. It seems they have been providing employment opportunities for prisoners, the same kind of prison labor our State Department once criticized China for using. Prisoners in Washington State have the chance to learn the garment trade through the efforts of Redwood Outdoors, Inc., a major supplier to Eddie Bauer. Prisoners are paid $4.90 an hour minus deductions for room and board, leaving them between $1.80 and $2.80 an hour. Even prisoners in Tennessee get to participate, producing novelty items like rocking horses. Eddie Bauer joins a growing list of elite companies such as Microsoft and AT&T that are availing themselves of the $1.4 billion prison industry. This is certainly "trendsetting" at its best.

New Work Environments

With shortages of labor cropping up, many other companies have been turning to our prison system and its world-record two million inmates. In the words of *The Wall Street Journal*, "economic reality and criminal justice intersect in America." Corporations were finding that parolees and inmates in halfway houses and drug abuse programs make good employees. Why? Because, said the *Journal* with a straight face, "Street and prison life, it turns out, aren't bad ways to prepare for certain jobs." A key reason for their success? "The parolees do so well in part because they are under tight supervision and risk returning to jail if they fail a drug test." Another vital lesson for managing our nation's workers.

Travel agencies, in particular, have been able to realize great savings by employing inmates. Travel Wholesalers International was booking trips for other travel agencies using a dozen female inmates from Leath Correctional Institution in South Carolina. Co-owner Daniel P. Bohan has discovered not only that our prisons are "filled with a lot of smart people," but that, "better yet, prison labor is cheap." How cheap? Try 50 cents an hour for starting salaries. And, says Mr. Bohan, "you don't even have to pay them benefits." Fortunately, our Mr. Bohan was wearing a drool protector when he said this. TransWorld Airlines was so inspired by this prisoner rehabilitation project, it went one step further. TWA opened an airline reservation center inside a youth detention center in Ventura, California.

Best Downsizings of an Individual

Here are our nominees for the best firings — in the corporate division. Up first is the manager of a 7-Eleven in Odessa, Texas, named Wiley Bergren. Wiley caught a teen-aged thief in his store, tied him up with a trash bag, and called the police. Not only was Mr. Bergren hailed as a hero, the next day he was treated to pizza and awards at a company-sponsored lunch for his efforts to increase sales. Then hours later he was, of course, fired. Mr. Bergren had violated company policy when he apprehended the thief, and the Southland Corporation (owners of 7-Eleven) has a very strict and clearly stated policy about not interfering in attempted robberies. Margaret Chabris, a spokesperson for Southland, said in a statement that had mid-echelon managers across the country cheering, "If you have a policy, you have to stick by it." Absolutely, otherwise why have policies? Just think of the wastage of paper.

Our next candidate, Kevin Gardner, had a similar experience in Spokane, Washington, after he risked his life to save a woman being chased by a man wielding a knife. His actions too violated company policy, and big time, because Mr. Gardner's primary duty was guarding a Loomis armored truck. By rescuing the woman, argued Loomis, he had endangered the safety of the property entrusted to him. Fortunately, the State Supreme Court ruled that Loomis' rules ran counter to state policies favoring life over property. But dissenting from this view was Chief Justice Barbara Madsen, who argued that a work rule requiring drivers to remain in their trucks was vital to protecting property. Judge Madsen did not expound on whether penalties should be increased if a driver saves multiple lives.

BEST FIRINGS BY A PUBLIC AGENCY

We turn now to the public sector where our first nominee is the Postal Service in White Plains, New York, for firing 18-year veteran letter carrier Martha Cherry for taking her rounds too slowly. This is what her supervisor had to say: "At each step, the heel of your leading foot did not pass the toe of the trailing foot by more than one inch. As a result, you required 13 minutes longer than your demonstrated ability to deliver mail to this section of your route." It was not reported whether other employees turned in Ms. Cherry or whether the supervisor had gotten down on his or her knees to measure the offending steps. Meanwhile the post office announced no progress in their investigation of why so many of their employees were "going postal."

Our second candidate is the King County Parks Department in Washington State. They've earned our praise for discovering a new reason for firing employees: overworking. The Parks Department suspended Helen Stanwell for working too much after she dared to work over her allotted 40 hours a week without additional compensation. She was caught red-handed by the Parks Manager, Bobbi Wallace, who reported in a manner befitting Sherlock Holmes, "you were seen working on August 22, 1996, after 6:00 PM." Ms. Stanwell confessed to having stayed late to look at a trail with a client without authorization. Wallace stated her actions displayed "dishonesty, insubordination, and a violation of the law." Ms. Stanwell had previously been suspended for three days for "poor communication skills" after sending a memo in response to a manager's request for cost-cutting ideas. She had suggested cutting nepotism. Tsk, tsk. Very poor communication skills indeed.

new ways to raise productivity

Enough about firings — we now turn to more positive news. According to administrative law judge Charles Schaefer, managers at Kentucky Fried Chicken discovered a new way to motivate workers. But as with many innovations, workers sometimes fail to appreciate all that is being done for them. In Wisconsin, KFC employee June Lauer thought her boss was just talking dirty. He called women "bitches," suggested tattooing Colonel Sanders' face on women's breasts, and made fairly indiscreet references to sexual organs and oral sex. Tired of the assaults on her sensibilities, Ms. Lauer quit and later filed a lawsuit. That is when Judge Schaefer entered the picture to lay down a fundamental principle of American jurisprudence. He sided with the manager: Use of vulgar and obscene language and terms can serve to promote group solidarity." Those of you still slapping your forehead saying "Why didn't I think of that" may want to pause long enough to hear the judge's final shot. "To the extent that it was intended to promote this end," he said, "it would have been an effort to achieve a legitimate business goal." I suggest we all start practicing our racial slurs now. I'm told they are very motivating.

Helpful Hints

When dealing with an important corporation, always be polite. Don't be like Jonah Peretti. When Nike started a wonderful program to allow consumers to celebrate their "freedom to choose" by personalizing tennis shoes with a name or phrase, Jonah had to spoil the party. He mailed in his money and requested the word "Sweatshop" be added to his shoes. In an e-mail, Nike carefully explained his choice of words violated their policy of not printing "inappropriate slang." Jonah e-mailed back, telling Nike that he shared their love of free expression, but that according to Webster's, the term "sweatshop" was considered proper English, its use dating back to 1892. Finally he offered a face-saving compromise — requesting a picture of the ten-year-old Vietnamese girl who had made his shoes. Very inappropriate. Naturally, news of Jonah's correspondence spread on the Internet like a virus, causing untold embarrassment to Nike and encouraging other politeness-challenged rabblerousers.

Corporate-Speak

WITH THE DOWNSIZING of governments and long droughts in our fight against foreign Evil, much of the responsibility for producing quality Newspeak has fallen on the shoulders of American corporations. After years of using nation-states as training wheels, our corporations finally demonstrated they're able to ride over us all on their own. It's been a real pleasure to watch how they've risen to the challenge of globalization while still being acting as neighborhood friends (I take ads seriously). By the year 2000, multinational corporations made up 51 of the 100 largest economies in the world. Leading CEOs like Bill Gates found themselves treated openly like heads of state when they visited foreign countries, especially when his net worth exceeds the local nation's gross national product. Anyway, bon voyage and thanks for letting us keep some of our quaint native customs like voting and paying taxes.

CEO PIONEER AWARDS

A *Business Week* survey found that by 1999, CEOs of large corporations made 475 times what the average employee made. In 1990, the difference had been a mere 84 times. This mushrooing inflation at the top produced tough competition for the Newspeak CEO Pioneer Award. How do you not give it to AT&T's Richard Allen for firing 40,000 workers and then raising his own salary? But no, the highly coveted award went to a surprise dark horse candidate, the CEO of the Investment Technology Group, Raymond L. Killian. While ITG's top executive, he pioneered new terrain in the all-important executive compensation category. In a company that employed only 125 people, had a total revenue of only $72 million, and ended the year losing $7.9 million, Mr. Killian managed to have himself paid $15.5 million including salary, stock options, and grants. Using a complicated formula well over my head, economist Graef Crystal estimated that, relative to company size and performance, Killian was overpaid an estimated 3,564%. That's a new record. To give some perspective, the runner-up in this division, Ralph Roberts of Triarc, was, by industry standards, only overpaid 2,037%. However, it turns out that the expense of paying these CEOs so exorbitantly is all worthwhile, at least according to Sears VP Bernard Brosky: "Making their lives pleasant and giving them what they want is a necessary situation." It's out of our control. The gods have spoken.

GLOBAL ATTITUDE ADJUSTMENT TIME

The giant merger of Chrysler and Germany's Daimler-Benz led to a minor cultural problem that needed ironing out. Chrysler executives made about eight times what their German counterparts took in. Thus Richard J. Easten, the Chrysler CEO, raked in $16 million a year while Jürgen Schrempp, the Daimler-Benz CEO, made a paltry $1.9 million. The obvious solution of raising the German salaries ran into the nagging problem of German attitudes against high executive pay and widening gaps between rich and poor. Explained Jeorg Pluta, director of the German Shareholder Protection Association: "It's the European mentality. The enrichment of an individual on the backs of workers is considered exploitation." That European mentality thing again. Thank God we gained our independence from them.

New-age CEOs

Our nation's top executives appear to be going beyond materialistic demands, displaying a newfound interest in holistic health. Much like Mafia wannabes who yearned to become "made men," CEOs now speak of wanting to be made "whole." Apparently executives can be made "whole" by being offered stock options by a prospective employer that compensates them for the stock they lose when jumping ship. For example, when Quaker Oats lured away Sprint's CEO Robert Lemay, they made him "whole" with $2.5 million in cash and $11.7 million in stock options. But apparently there are different levels of "wholeness" that executives can aspire to. So when Sprint replied with a $20.5-million package, it was, said a spokesperson, an effort to "make him a little more whole." I like this usage. Finally we have an objective way of measuring what it takes to make any person "whole" that leaves aside messy psychological categories. But it does raise the question of what it would cost to make the rest of us "whole." I can just hear it now: "Mr. Grytting, we have a $49 boom box for you. You are now whole."

Who Do You Trust?

A study by two social scientists, Shaheen Borna and James Stearns, found that convicts expressed higher ethical standards than a similar group of executives with MBAs. The pair quizzed 300 prisoners in a minimum-security facility and a like number of MBAs (not at the facility). They found, for example, that 73% of the MBAs admitted they would hire an employee from a rival company to gain trade secrets while only 60% of the prisoners said they'd do the same. In general, MBAs put shareholders first while convicts sided with the customers. It's hoped the results will not hurt employment chances for parolees.

Corporate Crime Report

While the FBI reported huge drops in crime, the trend was reversed in the flourishing field of corporate crime. *Fortune* reports that since 1982, federal fraud convictions have grown by more than 50%. They speculate that such crimes are increasing not only because of the global economic turmoil but because of "reduced corporate loyalties" (gasp). However, there is a silver lining to this picture beyond an exploding market for surveillance by private investigators. A study of corporations convicted of crimes, conducted by David and Melissa Baucus, found an unexpected pattern of forgiveness. Between 1974 and 1983, corporations convicted of antitrust violations, employee discrimination, or the production of harmful products saw their sales growth lag behind. But the stock value of the same companies kept pace with that of their competitors. Yes, Wall Street forgives. There is a place for religious values in our society.

welFare MOTHers resPOND

Government aid to corporations finally found some able public defenders. Corporate trough feeding has been under attack even by Republicans after polling showed it third on the public's hate list just behind waste and fraud in government. But William Workman of the U.S. Chamber of Commerce has a timely warning about the loaded phrase "corporate welfare." "One man's corporate welfare," he says, "is another man's paycheck" (let's not forget trickle-down economics). So maybe we should find a better phrase than "corporate welfare." Fortunately, John Deluca, president of the Wine Institute, had been thinking about just this problem. He defended the Agriculture Department's Market Access Program, which funnels $100 million a year to needy firms like Miller Beer, Gallo Wine, and McDonald's so they can advertise abroad, because other countries do the same. His suggestion: "Corporate welfare should be renamed 'competitive equity'" It does have a nice ring to it. Joining the parade, treasury secretary Robert Rubin announced he also did not like the "corporate welfare" slogan and preferred it to be called, and let's all get this correct, "corporate tax-base broadening." Much more positive, don't you think? Please erase the offending slogan from your memory banks.

einstein to the rescue

It took a while but someone finally stood up to publicly defend the deferred compensation schemes of our top corporate executives. Tax lawyer Robert M. Fields not only defended them, he attacked the unfairness of the current system to the rich. While typical pension plans give workers a retirement benefit of 30% of their top wages, "top executives rarely receive a 30% pension benefit" because of the "populist tinkering" with the tax code. (That populist Congress won't leave anything alone.) That's why the deferred compensation plans, in Mr. Field's choice words, "simply maintain the relative equality between management and rank and file workers." Let's say your CEO is used to earning about 400 times what you make. He or she is accustomed to a certain lifestyle that is also 400 times beyond yours. So you can just imagine how grossly unfair it must feel to them upon retirement if you are getting a pension and they aren't. The "relative equality" just goes down the tubes — an obvious injustice.

"I Have a Dream" Dept.

Coca-Cola clearly found a visionary new leader in its chief executive, M. Douglas Ivester. In his first public speech, Ivester urged his fellow executives to "expand the horizons of our businesses, and the horizons of our thinking." To demonstrate expanded horizons, he told an audience of Coke managers that the typical person drinks only four ounces of soft drink out of an average of 64 ounces of liquids per day. "That still leaves our industry," said Ivester, "with 60 ounces to go after. Put another way — we're only tapping four 64ths of the opportunity." But why stop at 60 ounces? That quibble aside, what a sense of mission. Can't you see thousands of Coke executives raising their briefcases high in the air in unison and vowing to go after those remaining ounces, reclaiming them from the clutches of milk, fruit juice, and water? Can't you picture Mr. Ivester approaching the Pearly Gates and telling St. Peter, "I raised the consumption of our nutritionally valueless caffeinated sugar water by two whole ounces. I'm ready."

LOaN SHarKS GO respecTaBLe

Not only are Jim Palmer and the Money Store providing loans for poor people at 25% interest, but now a host of our leading corporations — like the Travelers Group, General Electric, Ford Motors, and Key Bank — are competing to supply money to those in need. In 1996, Ford made $2.8 billion — two thirds of their profit — from the practice now legitimized as "subprime lending." The unregulated business of providing poor people with credit at sky-high interest rates has grown into a $300-billion industry "serving" 50 million Americans who don't qualify for standard loans. Lenders like Key Bank have been real leaders in this field, closing 140 branch offices so they could concentrate on buying up other subprime lending companies. Keycorp CEO Henry Meyer says enthusiastically, "Our branches are now sales centers, and their goal is to sell, sell, sell." Even better is the news that middle-class people can now participate in loan sharking by buying packages of loans safely labeled "subordinate mortgage-backed securities." Remember, you are not loan sharking, you are simply purchasing SMBSs (we show our sophistication by just using the acronym). Only in America.

BeYOND BreaSTFeeDING

Nestle has been subject to an ongoing boycott for their role in persuading Third World women to give up breastfeeding for the more "modern" use of artificial infant formula. The World Health Organization credits this practice with a million and a half deaths a year, largely due to the exposure of babies to contaminated drinking water. Instead of voluntarily restricting their Third World advertising, Nestle found a worthy free-market solution, yet another "win-win" made possible by their purchase of a company called Perrier. They simply began marketing a bottled water called Pure Life to mothers in 20 Third World nations, thus solidifying the all-important mother-Nestle-baby bond. To top off their goodwill efforts, Nestle even joined the environmental movement, initiating a model educational effort in Lahore, Pakistan, where it has encouraged a local ad agency to sponsor a series of "awareness seminars" on the dangers of contaminated water. Keeping with its natural modesty, Nestle refrained from mentioning its role in funding the campaign.

MCCHILDCare

Business is taking an interest in the poor, thanks to the Welfare Reform Bill, which eliminated the word "nonprofit" from the requirements for childcare. The $3.8 billion a year the government spends on foster care for half a million children has drawn a flood of big corporations from Lockheed Martin to Youth Services International (established by the founder of Jiffy Lube). This opening of childcare to major corporations is described by its chief lobbyist, the head of the Au Clair School, Kenneth Mazik, as a minor adjustment that "levels the playing field." It's reassuring to know that Lockheed Martin will have a level playing field when competing against church groups. For-profit companies promise to introduce new efficiencies into foster care. For example, Youth Services International promises to reduce costs by having the children do more of the work. Child labor, I believe it's called. It's this kind of innovative thinking that makes the entry of airplane and auto lubing companies into childcare so necessary.

BaNK refuses To "Close"

After 70 years, the Bank of America branch in the small town of Pescadero, California, announced it would be closing its doors. This is the only bank for the small town of 500 people and its surrounding farming community, and the closure means bad news for the remaining small businesses. You can imagine the relief that swept through the town when the bank clarified the announcement of a closure. It turns out the Bank of America was not "closing" the branch after all. According to the *Los Angeles Times*, "the bank doesn't use the word 'closing'." Instead, they were "consolidating." As stated by a bank official named Radin, the shutting down of the Pescadero branch (as we'd say in Oldspeak) was "part of a 'fine-tuning' process at Bank of America, one that will lead to the consolidation ... of 120 branches in California this year." I'm sure people in Pescadero know just where they have been "fine-tuned."

DONUT FEVEr

In 1998, a disgruntled customer of Dunkin Donuts in Connecticut by the name of David Felton vented his displeasure with the company by putting up a website called www.dunkin-donuts.org, where other customers could voice their complaints. Unfortunately, Dunkin Donuts did not share Mr. Felton's enthusiasm for grass-roots participation and promptly sued him for using copyrighted words belonging to the corporation. After much negotiation, the two sides reached a peaceful settlement, and Dunkin Donuts agreed to buy the website. Most commendable were the corporation's motives for purchasing the site. In an official statement, Dunkin Donuts said it bought the site so the company could "more effectively capture the comments and inquiries that are being submitted by our customers." (I especially like their use of the word *capture*.) It just isn't the same as reading those complaints on someone else's website. Anyway, I do want any corporations who take offense at what I write to know that you can buy my website. It's a bargain, really.

SHarKS eaTING SHarKS DePT.

In Oregon, a group of consumers formed a coalition to protest the $7.9-billion buyout of a local power company, PacifiCorp, by the foreign-owned ScottishPower. Using language not often heard since the 1960s, spokesperson Ken Canon declared, "We do have the feeling as customers that we're being transacted. We're kind of an asset that is being bought and sold — the earning power of a utility — like forced labor." Mr. Canon, by the way, was speaking for the Industrial Customers of Northwest Utilities. Among the fellow victims of "forced labor": Boise Cascade, Weyerhauser, Boeing, Georgia-Pacific, Simpson Timber, Atlantic Richfield, Shell Oil, etc. ... Welcome y'all to life on the lower rungs of the corporate food chain.

MICROSPEAK VERSION 4.1

Microsoft displayed such an unerring talent for Newspeak that the Justice Deptartment was concerned they might gain a monopoly here too. Microsoft's rivalry with Netscape in the web browser field (the Explorers vs. the Navigators) led to a few casualties on the linguistic field. To get the latest in correct terminology, we turn to Microsoft's *Manual of Style for Technical Publications*, where we find the following instructions: "Avoid the term *navigate* to refer to moving from site to site, page to page within a site, or link to link on the Internet ... Instead use *explore* or *move through* to refer to sequentially moving from one link or site to another, or a similar neutral term describing the action." And now that Netscape has released its "Communicator," I think we'd all do well to find synonyms for the verb *to communicate*. Likewise, since America Online bought up Netscape, the term *online* might be jettisoned, although I do believe erasing *America* would be going too far.

HAPPY THOUGHTS

As part of Microsoft's renewed educational efforts, one of their finer vice-presidents, Bob Herbold, formerly of Proctor & Gamble, granted an interview and deftly answered the question of why Microsoft didn't just confess to having a monopoly on PC operating systems. First, Mr. Herbold made a telling reply by asking, "How do you define that word?" His profundity was met by that of his questioner who replied, "An overwhelming share." Herbold pointed out how weak this definition of the term *monopoly* was because "most people would define it with some negative aspects. Defining that term just as a high market share we don't think is appropriate. Most people, when they hear that word, they connect negative connotations with it." And that, boys and girls, is why Microsoft does not have a "monopoly."

Almost equaling Mr. Herbold's performance was executive Paul Maritz' testimony at the Microsoft antitrust trial over whether Windows and Internet Explorer were separate products. Mr. Maritz admitted that "in preparation for this trial," Microsoft had replaced the word *browser* in all its literature with the phrase *Internet technologies*. Now that is much clearer. And why drop the term browser? "We were concerned," said Maritz, "that *browser* might be misconstrued and taken out of context." I know those big words always get me mixed up. But not only is the word browser confusing, so is the term *market*. When the government prosecutor asked whether he tracked browser market share, Maritz gave a now-classic answer: "We did. But that doesn't imply there was what we considered a market there." Seventeen philosophers reportedly had heart attacks upon hearing his words.

Helpful Hints

Whenever you go to talk to corporations, dress appropriately. If you lack a power suit, why not come dressed as a Corporate Crime Fighting Chicken. Michael Moore reports that Crackers, the designated chicken for the show *TV Nation*, was a phenomenal success wherever he traveled in his Crimemobile. More than 30,000 corporate crime tips were received at Crackers' 800-number. The power you can wield in a chicken costume should be immediately apparent. Imagine phoning to get in the corporate door. If you are an ordinary person, the receptionist might report to the CEO, "Boss, there's a woman who wants to talk about our lack of inner city investments." Versus, "Boss, there's a Corporate Crime Fighting Chicken that wants to talk to you." Costume shops have a wide range of outfits to choose from that rent for about $50 a day. But before one can internalize bureaucratic or corporate mindsets, one must have been a child. It's a biological requirement. So speak to the child hidden behind the suit.

McHealth and Science-Mart

ONCE UPON A TIME, in a land far away, science and medicine were considered to be callings. They were viewed as valuable forms of service to the community. Doctors took an oath, the Hippocratic oath, vowing to enter any house to cure the sick — no matter how much wealth they possessed. Scientists won awards for bettering the lot of mankind. This was before they knew the meaning of big words like *franchising* and *profit maximization*. Today's practitioners are learning many other big words as they awaken to their places on medical and scientific assembly lines. Now when I walk into my local medical clinic, I have this uncontrollable urge to pass out little white Burger King hats to all the staff. I'm working on getting this impulse under control.

PHILIP MORRIS SEES THE LIGHT

After decades of sticking their heads in the sand about the hazards of tobacco, Philip Morris found a new tactic: promoting the benefits to society of premature deaths from smoking. A study produced for them by Arthur D. Little, one of the "foremost management consulting firms," found the early deaths of smokers have

103

"positive effects" for society that more than counteract the medical costs of treating smoking-induced cancer and other such tobacco-related diseases. This path-breaking research was limited to smoking in Czechoslovakia. It found that in 1999, despite incurring health care costs for dying smokers, the government still had a net gain of $147.1 million from smoking-related earnings. From these figures, the American Legacy Foundation calculated that the Czech government saved $1,227 per dead smoker. That's a pretty good return, as Philip Morris proudly informed government leaders in the Czech Republic.

Philip Morris came in for a flood of criticism and publicly apologized for the conclusions, which is too bad because the report makes fascinating reading. It is, as the authors state, "the result of the exercise of our best professional judgment." (Imagine what we'd get if they were having an off day). What makes the study such a model of American scholarship is the care taken to leave no stones unturned. Not only did the Arthur D. Little researchers find out precisely how much early deaths save on health care expenses, housing for the elderly, social security, and pensions (something we all wanted to know), they also uncovered savings from premature deaths in areas we non-experts would never dream to look. Who would think to look at the effect of smoking deaths on unemployment? These authors did, and they found that "replacing those who die early ... leads to savings in social benefits paid to the unemployed and in costs of re-training." A wonderful gift to society by smokers.

But it gets even better. The researchers, with obvious relish, note that when a smoker dies prematurely, the savings to the state for that year are "only one part of the positive effect." There's more to come. You need to look at all the other years the smoker would have lived had she or he not smoked, because, we are told, "the savings will therefore influence the public finance balance of smoking in future years." It's a gift that keeps on giving.

It is unfortunate Philip Morris had to suffer such bad publicity. The company, famous for its slogan "Today's teenager is tomorrows potential regular customer," has been working hard to spruce up its image. In one year they spent $100 million on charity alone. Of course, they spent $150 million on telling people about their charitable giving, but this 3-to-2 ratio is actually quite good for an American corporation.

SCIENTIFIC GROUNDSWELL

Lest you think that Philip Morris is alone in recognizing the benefits to society of early deaths, know that they are in good company. Four years ago, the state of Alabama arrived at similar conclusions in a report by their attorney general that escaped public notice. This story was covered, as far as I know, only by the *Opelika-Auburn News.* Alabama Attorney General Bill Pryor found that "smoking-related health costs are not excessive, because smokers die young." This breathtaking conclusion was the result of an 89-page report (with footnotes, I'm told). The Alabama study apparently was just the tip of the iceberg, because it pointed to even more studies that "show taxpayers actually save money in costs for nursing homes, insurance, pensions, and Social Security benefits because smokers die earlier than non-smokers."

For those of you inclined to think that reasoning in Alabama takes its own course, know that none less than State Farm Insurance followed the same line in a study defending sport utility vehicles. Their researchers reported the following: "Sport utility vehicles may actually save insurers money in a few accidents, by killing people who might otherwise have survived with serious injuries. Severe injuries tend to produce larger settlements than deaths." Sounds like public thanks are owed to SUV makers, too. Obviously, great minds work in the same circles.

CEREAL KILLERS

One of the finer scandals from the past was the revelation that in the 1940s, Quaker Oats and the Massachusetts Institute of Technology teamed up to feed radioactive cereal to developmentally disabled students in an effort to understand how oatmeal was absorbed into the body. But even juicier was MIT's defense of its action. Although only minute amounts of radiation were involved,

MIT had fed the kids nuked cereal without telling parents, while the children were only told they were to be members of the "Science Club." Breaking new ground, MIT noted that its researchers had "acted properly under then-existing standards." This news came as somewhat of a surprise to millions of senior citizens who had survived World War II without knowingly feeding any kids radioactive cereal. Many felt they had let down the "then-existing standards." I'm told the Former Southern Racist Sheriffs' Association highly applauded the guilt-free notion.

USED SCIENCE FOR SALE

Vital scientific research at colleges and universities has been made possible due to the largesse of major corporations. For example, the University of Maine's Lobster Institute, funded by the seafood industry, published a study showing that lobsters really don't suffer when boiled alive. And the Credit Research Center at Georgetown University, funded by 70 companies in the credit industry, produced a wonderful study showing just how debtors have been using U.S. Chapter 7 bankruptcy laws to escape paying their credit card debts. This latter study was particularly timely because, by a marvelous coincidence, Congress was considering legislation to eliminate such Chapter 7 bankruptcies. But can funding sources influence the results of scholarly studies? The Dean of Georgetown's business school, Kasra Ferdows, didn't think so, pointing out that his school's study "meets our general rules" for good research. Moreover, since the CRC was funded by approximately 70 companies, the Dean took "some comfort" in the fact that no one corporate interest would predominate. Sounds like the contemporary definition for objectivity.

"TWAS BRILLIG AND THE SLITHY TOVES ..."

Medical education finally made it into the 20th century with the announcement of a program in New York to pay hospitals not to train doctors. Citing an oversupply of physicians, Medicare began a Graduate Medical Education Project that would pay participating hospitals up to $100,000 a year for each intern they do not train. The treatment of doctors on the model of corn production was not lost on the eagle eyes of our nation's medical community, most of whom responded by asking, "How can I get in on it?" But one medical professor, Dr. Alan Hillman of the University of Pennsylvania, described it as "an amazing treatment of health care as a commodity." Pretty shocking. But then two sentences later he softened his criticism, admitting that "I really can't find any fault with it." (Nor could Alice once she had accepted the premises of Wonderland.) And why is an "oversupply" of doctors a bad thing? Because, said *The New York Times*, in an answer that led three supply-side economists to commit suicide, it "drives up medical costs."

BIG MaC HeaLTH care

Private hospital franchises have been growing at an explosive rate. One of the largest, Columbia Health Care, has 348 hospitals and 285,000 employees and has been involved in 35 to 50 takeovers a year. "It is a world," reported *The Wall Street Journal*, "in which diseases from cancer to diabetes to manic depression become profitable 'product lines' ..." Columbia, for example, is offering eight "product lines" for cancer, cardiology, diabetes, etc. Individual doctors are to be replaced by disease management programs that standardize treatment, thus allowing lower-priced health technicians to punch into a computer and to come up with treatment plans. Said co-founder Richard Rainwater, "Somebody has to do in the hospital business what McDonald's has done in fast foods and what Wal-Mart has done in the retailing business." This progress has had its critics. CHC hospitals are expected to turn a 20% profit every year and to reach that figure, some have turned to lopping off unnecessary luxuries like emergency care. But for bleeding heart liberals, CEO Richard Scott had a ready answer. "Is any fast food restaurant," he asks, "obligated to feed everyone who shows up?" Finally, the perfect yardstick for moral reasoning in our country.

affordable Health care

Tired of the assembly-line character of modern medical practice, a number of doctors have been pioneering a new direction: health clubs for the wealthy. For a modest $22,000 a year for a family of four, you can have a doctor who will make house calls even if you are out of town, manage all aspects of your health care, and, as an added bonus, call you a "client" instead of a "patient." One service, called MD2, will even travel to your favorite vacation spots and "scout" out the medical environment in advance. While some doctors defend this as part of the American Dream, others realize it may evoke class envy. Says MD2 founder Dr. Howard Maron, his service "unfortunately is at a price that's difficult for most people to afford." He then displays his true humanity by adding, "I wish it wasn't that way." So sad that the good doctor has no control over his prices.

General Hospital Goes Deluxe

If a personal doctor for $22,000 a year isn't enough for you, you may want to check out one of the dozen or so hospitals that have opened VIP suites. Now for a mere $2,000 a day, you can have waiters in tuxedos serving fine cuisine, you can have monogrammed bathrobes, mahogany antiques, and even a wet bar in your room. In addition to medical personnel, the hospitals have recruited staff from many of our top hotels to insure the finest service. This practice has raised the usual complaints about class inequities. Critics question whether hospitals reliant upon Medicare should be using public funds to cater to the rich. Fortunately, Jose Nunez, Director of the Methodist Hospital in Houston, had an effective answer for these spoilsports. Nunez pointed to the fundamental human rights of wealthy foreigners: "International patients have higher expectations. Many of these individuals are used to having servants, maids, butlers, and gardeners." Do you have the heart to deprive them? I don't think so. Methodist Hospital has 27 luxury rooms at the bargain price of $1,200 a night.

New-aGe HOSPITaL Care

As the medical profession continues its evolution from a calling or a public service into a business, yet another hospital has announced it can no longer provide free care to the uninsured (except, of course, in life-threatening emergencies). The Raritan Bay Medical Center in Trenton, New Jersey, in a slight amendment to the physicians' ancient Hippocratic Oath of service, declared it was the state's responsibility to cover the costs of those unable to pay, and closed its community health clinic. Most memorable was the statement of hospital President Keith McLaughlin, on the front page of *The New York Times*, no less: "Providing health care for those in need is not a hospital problem." I'm told the Raritan center will be posting signs directing the poor to local public libraries and Wal-Marts for medical care.

DOCTOrs FIND THeIr True CaLLING

Doctors saw their earnings plummet in the 1990s. They complained as HMOs turned them into mere "health care providers" whose services were to be sold at the lowest price possible. Doctors like Glenn Meyers of Florida, who had watched his income drop from $400,000 to a mere $300,000, said HMOs were "imperiling the lifestyle they expected." Fortunately, Dr. Meyers, like many others in the medical community, found an answer. He turned to Amway! Now when he meets patients stressed out from financial concerns, he can take them aside and offer a real cure selling everything from soap powders to appliances. Although doctors must be careful not to sell Amway products while practicing medicine (it would be bad taste during an operation), they can drop hints even to colleagues about the need to build a "hedge against managed care," and then suggest a private discussion later. More doctors are heeding the Amway call despite the unfortunate fact, reported by Dr. Don Berkowitz, that "a lot of doctors are scared that it reduces their status." But sometimes you just have to be a rebel.

"aND a Free Toaster WITH eaCH aPPeNDeCTOMY"

In Evanston, Illinois, women shoppers at Nordstrom's were
offered a tremendous bargain. They could have a mammogram
right in the store and not miss a minute of valuable shopping
time, plus get a free facial. *Business Week* reported that "years ago
such advertising and promotional gimmicks were considered
tacky and unprofessional." Now that we have outgrown such
antiquarian notions, doctors have been jumping on discounts and
freebies with a newfound zeal. In the understated words of Allan
Glick, a VP with HIP Health Plans of New York, there are "many
things we in health care have learned from our cousins in retailing." Now it sounds like the "cousins" may have some catching
up to do.

PSYCHO: THE aD

Drug companies have been dropping their practice of limiting the
advertising of prescription drugs to just medical professionals.
Even mental health drugs for depression and schizophrenia are
now being marketed directly to consumers. Alan Holmer, president of the Pharmaceutical Manufacturing Association, defended
this direct marketing to potentially unbalanced consumers in these
words: "This is the information age and more information
empowers patients to be able to have more meaningful conversations with their doctors about cures and treatments." Right on,
brother. I remember just how empowered I felt after watching my
first McDonald's commercial. Fortunately, according to *The Wall
Street Journal*, "There is no shortage of experts helping drug
companies learn to think more like a Coke or a Nike."

According to a study showing that 25% of the public has
changed physicians in the past two years, a steady relation with a
family doctor has gone the way of the rest of the memorabilia from
the1950s. Drug companies not only have the chance to step into
the "breach" between doctor and patient, reported Rachel
Weissman in *American Demographics*, but the "doctor-patient
relationship is being replaced by a drug marketer-patient bond." I
know I value my "bonds" with large multi-national corporations

and I'm sure the new found "relationships" will be just as satisfying as those once engaged in with actual human beings. Hear that, HAL?

auditors to the rescue

Investigators for the Department of Health and Human Services unearthed a grave wastage of federal money: terminally ill people who were not dying in their allotted time. Each year, hospices care for nearly 400,000 dying people. Medicare provides hospice benefits for people certified by their doctors as having no more than six months to live. But thousands of elderly people have lived longer than the six months granted them in Medicare's hospice program. DHHS wanted the return of $83-million spent on people who lived longer than their doctors certified they would. Said one elderly patient, "I just feel terrible because I am one of these people who cause the hospice problem. I would die if I could, but God just won't take me." Hospice director Mary Laback asks the critical question, "What do you do if people live too long?" To which the DHHS auditors reply that hospices shouldn't have "improperly spent $83-million caring for people ..." Thank goodness for professional objectivity.

WHITE GUMMY LIQUID DEPT.

One of the industries the World Trade Organization will have to consider regulating is the burgeoning trade in sperm. So far Denmark has emerged as the center of the $100-million-a-year mail-order business thanks to the vision of Ole Schou, CEO of the Cryos International Sperm Bank in Copenhagen. Schou not only wanted to be the best in the business, he had a Mt. Everest-size goal. "We think we can be," he said, "the McDonald's of sperm." I must admit that is one sentence I never dreamt I'd ever hear in my lifetime. For those of you overprone to humor, please do not ask about their "Happy Meal."

Helpful Hints

Among the many useful sites on the Internet is RTMark (www.rtmark.com), a site devoted to "the informative alteration of corporate products." RTMark is a meeting ground for people who have projects that would involve the "tactical embarrassment" of large organizations as well as for investors who'd like to see their money serve a socially useful purpose. An RTMark grant, for example, helped fund the fine work of the Barbie Liberation Organization. These are my personal favorite investment opportunities from the hundreds that have been offered at RTMark:

1. A project to rename a major chemical incineration plant after Ronald Reagan.
2. Lobbying for a rating system that ranks films and TV shows by the extent of product placements.
3. Five hundred dollar rewards to police officers who will "profile" white businessmen after 6:00 p.m..

It is the philosophy of RTMark that "by catching powerful entities off-guard, you can momentarily expose them to public scrutiny."

Legal Disorders

WITH AN ESTIMATED two million adults in prison, the United States leads the rest of the world in the prestigious prison race competition. With so many industries pulling up stakes and moving overseas, it's good to report on one that has remained loyal to America. With more lawyers than the Roman Empire had soldiers, we are ready for any emergency. I sleep calmly at night, secure in the knowledge that should any foreign foe try to invade us, our attorneys will sue their pants off in court. Meanwhile, judicial reasoning has been taking its own twists and turns, reflecting the value of having officials live removed from ordinary life, far off in a world of their own.

DEFENDING THE HOMELAND

Parents sometimes go too far in trying to protect their children. The state of Massachusetts had a law banning billboards with tobacco advertising from being placed within 1000 feet of a school. The U.S. Supreme Court ruled this ban abridged the tobacco companies' First Amendment rights to broadcast their message on every street corner. Justice Clarence Thomas showed he had fulfilled the "hopes" many had for him when he wrote, in a concurring opinion, "harmful products [like] harmful ideas are entitled to the protection of the First Amendment." Then Thomas served up his clincher argument: the Domino Theory. If we allow advertising bans on harmful products, he argued, "attacks on fast food would be next." I know it's a shocking prospect, but those activists will stop at nothing.

THE CON GOES ON

Do you worry about what happens to white-collar criminals once they leave prison? Now there's an organization willing to employ their talents — on the corporate lecture circuit. A speakers' agency called Pros and the Cons has been sending out a parade of convicted embezzlers like Whitewater figure Webster Hubbel to speak to corporations willing to pay $1000 or more for the edifying experience. That's a figure slightly higher than what blue-collar criminals can expect — let that be a lesson to them. Part of the reason for this disparity is explained by *The Wall Street Journal* in an observation about Barry Minkow, an embezzler of $26 million: "The very attributes that enabled Mr. Minkow to hoodwink sophisticated bankers and private investors — charm, aplomb, ingenuity — served him well as a speaker." Apparently corporate audiences are more comfortable with someone who speaks their language.

McPRISON RAISES ITS STANDARDS

While firms like Columbia have worked spreading the McDonald's gospel in the hospital industry, Corrections Corporation of America has quietly emerged as the fast food king of private prisons. CCA, worth $3.5 billion, has been among the top five performing stocks on the New York Stock Exchange. It accounted for nearly half of the 77,000 prisoners who were incarcerated by private corporations in 1997. Much of this success is due to the philosophy of co-founder Thomas Beasley, who says that in the prison business, "You just sell it like you were selling cars or real estate or hamburgers." This refreshing candor has of course invited criticism that private prisons cut too many corners and lower their standards to increase profits. Fortunately, a spokeswoman for CCA named Susan Hart has shown that the high standards of our penal system are being upheld, at least in their hiring practices for guards. In her words: "It would be inappropriate, for certain positions, [to hire] someone who said, 'Yes, I beat a prisoner to death.' That would be a red flag for us." But just for "certain positions" ...

reTUrN OF THE KEYSTONE COPS

Two inmates in a Texas private jail discovered a rather large legal loophole after they had escaped from prison only to be recaptured 11 days later. Authorities found they couldn't prosecute the men for escaping. Texas is on the cutting edge of a great growth industry: private for-profit prisons. But under Texas law, the guards at these facilities are not classified as peace officers or public servants. Thus, reasoned county prosecutor John Holmes, the prisoners could not have committed the offense of escape. Similarly the state of Oregon, where the prisoners had been exported from, reasoned they could not prosecute because the escape had occurred in Texas. State officials in Texas are, as I write, still trying to figure out whom to bill for tracking down the non-escapees.

NEW STANDARDS FOR PUNISHMENT

When convicted killer Pedro Medina was electrocuted in Florida, a mask covering his face burst into flames. This brought on a lot of criticism and a promise by Gov. Lawton Chiles to look at other methods of execution. But not every official in Florida caved in to liberal pressure groups. Attorney General Bob Butterworth had this humane comment: "People who wish to commit murder, they better not do it in the state of Florida because we may have a problem with our electric chair." But Florida Senate Majority Leader Locke Burke went a step further and put forward a profound philosophy of punishment. He complained that the more common method of injecting poison "appears to be a medical procedure." Not good enough for Florida. "A painless death," he announced, "is not punishment." But being forced to listen to this Senator certainly would be — cruel and unusual punishment.

UPHOLDING COMMUNITY STANDARDS

A judge in New York settled one of the age's most burning questions when he officially ruled that men's breasts are not as erotic as women's. Judge John S. Martin's vital discovery that women's breasts have more sex appeal came in a case challenging the city's 1995 law banning topless bars in residential areas. Attorneys for the Cozy Cabin dancing establishment argued sex discrimination because the law does not bar men from baring their chests even though "male pecs are sexually arousing," according to psychologist Lenore Tiefer, who pointed to a popular Diet Coke commercial showing women turned on by a shirtless construction worker. But the judge ruled that "if ten topless women were walking down Park Avenue and ten topless men were walking down Madison Avenue, the effect on the traffic on Park Avenue would be substantially greater than that on Madison Avenue." Thus the judge established a new traffic-stopping standard for judging obscenity. Unfortunately, the ruling would seem to have left open the status of topless women who do not stop traffic on Park Avenue. Can they safely dance topless? How would Judge Martin handle that?

NO FREE LUNCH DEPT.

In Florida, a state court ruled that prisons may charge money for meals and medicine, thus allowing the Marion County jail to continue their innovative program of teaching economics to prisoners. This was an important victory for the county's program because, said Sheriff Ken Ergle, "We're not some backwoods, seat-of-the-pants operation." No, the Marion County approach had one very unique element of fairness that showcased its modernity. Prisoners in the 13,000-bed facility were allowed to pay for their meals whether they were guilty or not. The soft-hearted notion that prisoners being held for trial who are later found innocent shouldn't have to pay for their incarceration is easily dealt with by Sheriff Ergle. "If you're in jail, he said, "it's because you went in the initial stages of due process and a judge found there was reason to hold you. Even if you were found innocent, you were still lawfully and legally detained." It's all done by the book. Just ask Ken Kesey's Nurse Ratched.

WILDERNESS JUSTICE RETURNS

Louisiana declared open season on carjackers, allowing owners of autos a year-round hunting season against anyone threatening their property. The property protection bill thoughtfully allows the state's upstanding citizens to shoot miscreants with their handguns, but also their squirrel guns or assault rifles. (Howitzers and antitank weapons were inexplicably left out.) The bill declares "deadly force justified" when committed against a person "reasonably believed" to be making an unlawful entry. If we want to fully appreciate the mood of Louisiana's lawmakers, we should know that the word *reasonably* was not in the original bill. However, this obvious liberal addendum to the term *believed* failed to water down the legislation. Its intent was best captured by the stirring words of a Republican candidate for governor in Georgia named Michael Bowers: "Carjackers shot dead won't be carjacking anyone else." So true. And likewise, jaywalkers shot dead won't be ...

HAVING YOUR CAKE AND EATING IT TOO

Lawyers who opposed the tobacco industry in the historic $382-billion tobacco lawsuit did not go unrewarded for their efforts, as many of us had feared. Arbitrators awarded them a tidy $8.2 billion. While critics blasted their greed in claiming outrageous fees at the same time the clients they represented were dying of lung cancer, the attorneys themselves presented strong defenses for the multimillions earned by their firms. Among the better crop of rationalizations was that of attorney Richard Scruggs, thanks to the settlement, owner of a brand-new $192,000 Bentley. He argued that if the tobacco companies hadn't found their requests reasonable, "they would not have paid them so much." Besides, the tobacco companies had agreed to pay in "like kind and character as the industry pays its own lawyers and consultants." This included expenses like $250,000 for Florida attorney Robert Kerrigan to fly his private jet. Now let's see if we have this straight.

First you show that an industry is corrupt, and then you hold up that industry's judgment of what is "reasonable" to defend your new Bentley.

John Calhoun Wells, chair of the arbitration panel that determined the fees, noted that without the lawyers "there would be no multi-billion settlement for the states ..." I mean imagine the embarrassment to the states if no lawyers had shown up because, say, only a billion dollars had been offered. Attorney Joseph Rice, whose firm earned a cool one billion dollars for two years of work, asked, "Why should the lawyers who carried the burden and led the fight not be paid like a chief executive officer of a corporation?" As if executive pay were now our model of fairness in society. Then there is the elegant simplicity of attorney Robert Kerrigan's answer after he had been awarded $200 million for his work: "It sounds fair to me." I'm sure it did.

Letter of the Law Dept.

New York City passed a tough ordinance stopping adult strip clubs from operating in most of the city by outlawing them from operating within 500 feet of any school, home, or daycare center. One enterprising club, Ten's World Class Cabaret in Manhattan, read the ordinance and then attempted to sidestep the closure by becoming a non-"adults-only" strip club. Great joke. Let the kids in too, and the law doesn't apply. Ha, ha. But those still chuckling hadn't counted on the legal sagacity of state Supreme Court Justice Stephen Crane, who struck a blow for sticking to the precise wording of the law regardless of any intent. Granted, the law stomped all over the First Amendment. But it was clearly intended to protect children from exposure to bare-chested women and dirty old men in trench coats. Despite having a law in front of him barring stripping within 500 feet of any potential child, the judge agreed that Ten's "cannot be defined as an adult eating and drinking establishment if it does not exclude minors." Could it be the right wing was right about the dangers of fluoride in our drinking water after all?

Bureaucracy in action

A near tragedy struck the Seattle Police Department as two members of the fingerprint identification section fell off their chairs and injured themselves. The chairs were on rollers and were confiscated immediately. The good news is that the chairs will be returned after all members of the unit receive instruction on how to use them properly. A memo entitled "Chairs/sitting" advised employees of the following: "Until the safety officer can come down and give formal training, please inform all of your employees to take hold of the arms and get control of the chair before sitting down." I cannot emphasize how important these words are. If your workplace does not have a safety program in place to teach proper chair sitting, send now for our new publication *The Seven Habits of Highly Effective Chair Sitters.*

The Naked City

A class-action lawsuit was brought against the city of New York on behalf of 63,000 citizens who were illegally strip-searched during 1996 and 1997. To the city's credit, the searches were halted in 1997, only ten years after the U.S. Supreme Court had ruled that stripping people's clothes off during investigations of minor offenses was unconstitutional. A spokesperson for New York's legal department, Lorna Goodman, stepped forward to clarify what had gone awry. "This was not a policy," said Goodman. "This was a mistake." End of story — thanks, I presume, to a meticulous investigation of these cases. Can't you just picture a crack team of lawyers reviewing each of the files of the 63,000 strip-searches and saying after each one, "Oops, a mistake. Oops, a mistake. Oops, another mistake ...">

Cool Hand Luke Update

Massachusetts stole a leaf from Alabama's penal practices and initiated its first chain gang. While armed guards watched, prisoners shackled by the ankles painted fences out in the community. However, showing how trend-setting the northern state is, officials did not refer to the chain gangs by that time-honored name. Bristol

County Sheriff Thomas Hodgson said his department preferred the term "tandem work crews". "Chain gangs were meant to break people down," said Sheriff Hodgson. "My program is the complete opposite — it builds self-esteem and self confidence, and helps them know they've accomplished something." Absolutely. Can't you just hear prisoners telling people strolling past that they're just out building up their self-esteem by being shackled together in public? And why limit a program with such obvious benefits to prisoners? What about students? Don't they need their self-esteem boosted too?

NOT ALL GOD'S CHILDREN

In Texas a divorced lesbian mother ran afoul of the law when she took her five-year-old daughter to the Metropolitan Community Church, a congregation that engaged in ministry to gays and lesbians. Her ex-husband objected and took her to court, where he found a like-minded soul in Judge Keith Nelson. The Wichita County judge ruled the couple's divorce agreement, allowing the child to be raised in both the Christian and Jewish faiths, implied the child would attend a "mainline church." Naturally, the lesbian-friendly church was not on his "mainline" list. For those of you concerned about maintaining a proper level of conformity, here is his official list of approved churches: "Catholic church, churches of the Protestant faith, such as Presbyterian, Methodist, Baptist, Christian, Episcopalian, and the like ..." As if we would all just naturally know what "the like" is?

GLOBAL JAIL

The fear of prisoners escaping their confinement has been solved by a simple expedient: using the entire earth as a prison. New surveillance technology employing global positioning satellites (GPSs) and wireless modules worn on ankles may allow for complete monitoring of offenders anywhere on the planet. Leading edge companies in the surveillance field, like ProTech Monitoring, are excited about the possibilities of their "offender satellite surveillance system." Said PTM president Bob Martinez, "Our business aims at taking offender monitoring into the 21st century."

This enthusiasm is echoed by Jason Coheneur, sales VP for Sierra Wireless, who praises his company's "continued strategy to deliver practical, effective wireless solutions to new segments of the public safety market." Hoyt Layson, VP for PTM, praises his company's products as "the perfect option for our complete wireless solution." Such enthusiasm for utilizing a formerly wasted resource — the world — as a prison.

SUPPORT YOUR LOCAL FEDERAL JUDGE

The U.S. Supreme Court stepped in to protect yet another oppressed group, saving 16 Federal judges from having to pay increases in Medicare and Social Security. The Founding Fathers were very clear that judges' compensation "shall not be diminished during continuance in office." They were no dummies. So in 1989, the set of all alert lifetime judges banded together to sue the government, contending that new taxes instituted in 1983, when they were all on the bench, had "unlawfully diminished their salaries ..." But the best part is still to come. Continuing their argument, they added the clause, "thereby threatening judicial independence." Apparently the higher level of taxation only affected the independence of those judges placed in office before 1983, because judges appointed afterwards (presumably a more rugged lot) were not allowed to join the club. If Federal judges who make well in excess of $100,000 a year can have their independence threatened so easily, what does that say about the impact of taxes on us peons? A dangerous precedent.

WRONG TURNS

David Weisenthal, also known as Havana Dave, brought 100 duty-free cigars back from Cuba after having faithfully followed instructions from a U.S. Customs publication entitled *Know Before You Go*. For his efforts, he had all his cigars confiscated. Let's see where Dave went wrong. This is how, according to Judge Dalzell of the U.S. District Court of Eastern Pennsylvania, he failed to follow procedures:

1. Even though the Customs book said in "plain language" that 100 or less cigars could enter the country duty free, Dave had relied on information from the wrong agency. He came under the Regulations of the Office of Foreign Assets Control.
2. Dave responded that OFAC had issued no "instructions" to follow. To this the court said Dave "gave OFAC more credit than the agency was due when assuming mention of 'instruction' [in their Regulations] meant that OFAC actually would issue an instruction from time to time."
3. The bottom line: Dave's defense failed, said the judge, because "it is only supported by common sense." If this makes no sense, try rereading *Alice in Wonderland*.

WHY I WaNT TO Be a LaWYer

In a highly competitive field, Houston attorney George Fleming won top honors for bringing chutzpah to new heights in the legal field. Mr. Fleming set a record when he demanded as his legal fee $108.8 million out of a $170 million settlement against Shell Oil and Dupont for the failure of plumbing materials. He figured out this amount by adding to his 40% contingency fee $20 million in expenses and 40% of the discounted value of the new plumbing for his 37,000 clients. Now bear with me through some legalese. Even with so many clients, Mr. Fleming believed this was not a class-action law suit, an important point because lawyer fees in class actions are much lower than the 40% Mr. Fleming felt entitled to, often under 10%. He argued his case was not a class-action lawsuit because, get this, "he had treated each client as an individual." All 37,000.

Helpful Hints

Students can play a vital role in the campaign to save us from drowning in Newspeak. Sitting right in your classroom are the Newspeakers of tomorrow. Get together with trusted friends and set up an Early Warning System. Learn the Seven Signs of Psychic Numbing, among which are these sure-fire indicators:

1. Student continually raises hand to ask, "Will that be on the final exam?"
2. Student carries a "personal planner" and requires friends to make appointments.
3. Student associates exclusively with popular rich kids and shows signs of brown stains on nose.
4. Student talks about investment planning and retirement accounts.

Once your group has reached a consensus about the target, develop an action plan to effectively subvert the budding Newspeaker's worldview. The sixties-style sex, drugs, and rock 'n roll strategy is definitely passé. Turned out to be a bit shallow. Here are some more productive first steps:

1. A solid week of backpacking through the Cascade Mountains.
2. Volunteering as a tutor in the inner city or as a helper at a foodbank.
3. A silent meditation retreat without TVs, laptops, or cell phones.
4. A volunteer service vacation to a Third World country.

All of this can help in the vital deprogramming of a future corporate ladder climber.

Big Brotherdom

S URVEILLANCE WAS ONCE treated by the government as its own private property. But modern technological advances are allowing everyone to get in on the act. The spread of corporate "little brothers" was the big story until the feds retook the lead with a big splash after September 11th. Just as impressive have been the "improvements" in attitudes about being watched and tracked continuously. Beyond the patriotism that has fueled a renewed invasion of privacy is another strain of Americana best shown by the motto proudly displayed in Subway sandwich shops across the country: "Smile, you are being videotaped." Be happy. Compare this to George Orwell's lumbering slogan, "Big Brother is Watching You" — and you'll appreciate how far we've come.

MAKING A BETTER WORLD

For those who wondered how to help their country after the terrorist attacks of September 11th, there were these helpful words from military consultant Loren B. Thompson. As he told the readers of *The Wall Street Journal*, the "most valuable tool of domestic counterterrorism is a mistrustful citizenry." We need, he said, to encourage "skepticism about strangers." The prayers of citizens like Thompson were put into law with the passage of the USA Patriot Act, which freed the government to use its stockpiles of surveillance equipment without being stuck with time-consuming paperwork.

Knee-jerk civil libertarians failed to appreciate some of the accomplishments of the Patriot Act. The ACLU estimated it violated not just one but six amendments in the Bill of Rights (the first, fourth, fifth, sixth, eighth, and thirteenth), setting a modern day record (how it missed the second, third, seventh, and ninth is still being debated). Just as importantly, the Act managed to "update" our concept of "domestic terrorism." Not content to limit terrorism to actions that threaten human life, the Act added the all-important category of actions that "appear to be intended ... to influence the policy of a government by intimidation or coercion." In one fell swoop, the Act managed something no other piece of legislation has ever attempted: linking together Patrick Henry, Thomas Jefferson, the Boston Tea Party, the civil rights movement, the suffragettes, the labor movement, the peace movement — as the domestic terrorists they obviously were.

Having nothing better to do, I went to my dictionary and looked up the meaning of "intimidation." Here it is from *Merriam-Webster*: intimidation "implies inducing fear or a sense of inferiority into another." Very few commentators have appreciated our national interest in protecting government officials from a sense of inferiority. Nor have they noted that the Act's definition of terrorism is not limited to actions against our government, but towards "a government." Which introduces a ticklish problem for us as taxpayers. On this reading, we could be held responsible for our military's efforts to intimidate another government.

As for critics of the Patriotism Act, Attorney General John Ashcroft had this timely warning: "To those who scare peace-loving people with phantoms of lost liberty, my message is this: Your tactics only aid terrorists." Criticism of the Bush administration, he added, just "gives ammunition to America's enemies and pause to America's friends." A perfect circle, just like in the Inquisition of the Middle Ages, where questioning the right to torture was sure evidence of one's bewitchment or heresy. It leaves us with only one possible course of action: Let's pick a day and turn ourselves in as terrorists. Whether as satirists inducing inferiority or as taxpayers, we're all guilty. Let's save the government the expense.

THE BLIND LEADING THE BLIND

Among those who have been faithfully checking under their beds at night has been Lynne Cheney, wife to the Vice-President, who heads an organization called the American Council of Trustees and Alumni. This organization entered the forefront of groups defending the security of our nation with the timely publication of a study called *Defending Civilization: How Our Universities Are Failing America and What You Can Do About It*. The study reports that historically, "when a nation's intellectuals are unwilling to defend its civilization, they give comfort to its adversaries." Citing the names of 117 academics who have been inadequately patriotic, the study concludes that "college and university faculty have been the weak link in America's response to the attack."

I'm betting most history professors have had no clue how important their writings are to America's security. Among my personal favorites of those placed on the blacklist was the academic (whom we'll leave anonymous) included for quoting just one sentence from Martin Luther King Jr.: "An eye for an eye leaves the whole world blind." Very suspect. Let's get out the search warrants.

ATTITUDE ADJUSTMENT TIME

Are you fearful of the government's use of electronic surveillance? Do you have nightmares about seedy-looking FBI agents staying up late monitoring your e-mail? Well, you may be harboring "extremist" and even "elitist" and "nondemocratic" views. So warned the FBI's Alan McDonald about critics of the government's electronic surveillance who are threatening the nation's security by making normal law enforcement more difficult. Undoubtedly, you are wondering whether your own unreasoning paranoia can be overcome. "Yes," said McDonald. It's so simple: "When people don't know much about electronic surveillance, they are fearful of it. But when they know Congress passed laws and the Supreme Court reviewed them and that there are numerous constraints and procedures, then it makes sense to them. It seems rational and balanced." Just the knowledge that Congress was involved certainly removed my fears.

New Wine in Old Wine Bags Dept.

The FBI unveiled a new name for their Internet surveillance software formerly known as Carnivore. The software, when connected to an Internet service provider's network, allows the FBI to read a suspect's e-mail and follow their web surfing. According to FBI spokesperson Paul Bresson, the somewhat predatory name Carnivore was found to bring up "unfortunate" images for citizens. (Note that it did not seem to bring up such images for the Bureau officials.) Said Bresson, "With upgrades come new names." So the FBI put its most creative talents, I presume, to work and came up with a new title: DCS1000! And what does it mean, you ask? Bresson admits it "doesn't stand for anything." It's just an empty name, as empty as ... (Would you mind completing this sentence for me?)

Son of Star Wars

The Pentagon unveiled a new heat ray gun designed to disperse crowds without harming them permanently. The gun shoots electromagnetic energy able to produce burning sensations, without really burning the targeted bodies. The Pentagon touts it as a perfectly safe form of crowd control (particularly with crowds that include elderly people, children, and pregnant women, I would guess). This microwave gun was given a name that destined it for greatness. The Defense Department called it an "active denial system." Surprisingly, the phrase "active denial system" is the very same phrase used by some very cynical people to describe the Pentagon. Life is full of coincidences.

rent a spy satellite

Commercial spy satellites have become available to large corporations and small countries alike. Earthwatch Inc. launched the first of a dozen spy satellites capable of photographing garbage cans from space. "The possibilities are endless," said optimistic Earthwatch spokespeople, who predicted the market for surveillance could reach billions of dollars annually. The federal government kindly approved the use of spy technology by industry to help our struggling defense companies "challenge foreign rivals in the emerging industry of civilian surveillance from space." (Gotta keep up with the Joneses.) Against critics who warn of a massive invasion of privacy comes this gem of a defense by space issues lawyer Joanne Gabrynowicz. "We fought the Cold War," she argued, "to prove that open-information societies are better than closed ones. We can't stop now." Let's play with that sentence a bit. We fought communism so that IBM and Texaco could watch me in a hot tub in my back yard? I don't think we got our money's worth. This is the "open society?" All I can say is, as a public service, I'm keeping my fly zipped at all times.

DO-IT-Yourself SPY KITS

Is productivity lagging at your company? Well, ABC Asia Pacific may have the answer. For those who can't afford their own spy satellites, spy cameras are available for only $2,200 apiece. And for a limited time only, you could actually buy one and get the second one free. Said ABC Asia Pacific CEO Jeffrey Tan, "Productivity really does go up with this system. You see a very quick return on your investment in any business." Not only will installing the Spy Eyes system act as a deterrent to theft, but Mr. Tan reports it can help managers see if employees are really working and so "reduce unjustified management complaints." This is bound to make it equally popular with workers. Summing up, Tan says that it's "a helpful tool for people who want to stay in control." I'm told it's as popular with dominatrixes as it is with management.

BIG BROTHER VISITS THE WASHROOM

Corporations can ensure their employees have clean hands thanks to an invention called Hygiene Guard. For a mere $1,500, Hygiene Guard can be installed in any washroom. Employees need only wear a small badge. When they enter the restroom, an infrared sensor is triggered. A second sensor at the washstand is triggered if the employee stands in front of it for at least 15 seconds. This information is then relayed to a computer. Failure to use the soap dispenser causes the badge to blink, alerting all to the unhygienic behavior. NetTech International says this system would alert employers to "miscreants who don't enter the lavatory all day or use it too much." They could, I suspect, even draw up and post graphs of employee bathroom use with the "miscreants" posted in red. Obviously this is just the beginning. The mind reels at the possibilities. How about those people who waste company toilet paper? A serious problem. NetTech CEO Glenn Cohen defends their invention on public health grounds, actually declaring, "Our belief is it's time for Big Brother to be concerned." Well, he is, Glenn.

LITTLE BROTHERS ON THE NET

Thanks to software developed by Sequel Technology, corporations are now able to monitor where their employees travel on the Internet. Not only can their software tell a company when and where you go online, but it can also block "unapproved sites" like www.Playboy.com. Critics like Marc Rotenberg, director of the Electronic Privacy Information Center, say that it's "one thing to say 'no reading on the job' but quite another to say 'let me see what you're reading'." But Sequel Technology president Stuart Rosove has a rebuttal for such whiners. He claims that his software is not designed for spying: "This is not to dictate how people use the Internet, but for companies to set a best-use policy and use the software to enforce it." I just wish someone had been there to set a best-use policy for me. Could have saved me from reading Mr. Rosove's statement and almost losing my lunch. But setting a "best-use" policy is certainly an advance over crude censorship. Just take one Darvon and you'll feel better about this.

SMILE aND SHUT UP DEPT.

The debate over privacy on the Internet finally came to an end thanks to the timely intervention of Sun Microsystem CEO Scott McNealy. At a news conference, he introduced his company's latest software, called Jini, designed to integrate networks of computers and video and audio sources. To do so, it assigns unique numbers so each computer can be readily identified just as Intel and all our better software companies are doing. Silencing worries that this may open the door to the total surveillance of computer usage, McNealy presented the clincher argument that lesser minds had overlooked. "You already have zero privacy," he growled, "get over it." His staff is reportedly hard at work on a line of corollaries to this reasoning, such as "You're already getting ripped off — get over it" and even bringing back the ever-popular British slogan from the Boston Tea Party, "You're already overtaxed — get over it."

Advancing even further was Stefan Tornquist, marketing director at Bluestreak.com Inc., an on-line marketing firm offering technology that tracks traffic at websites using "cookies" able to brand a user's computer. Referring to programs that allow individuals to block cookies, Mr. Tornquist lamented that the "average consumer doesn't understand what they're giving up when they block cookies." Ah for the joys of targeted advertising. Then he expressed the modern day sensibility toward surveillance. "Today's invasion of privacy," he proclaimed, "is tomorrow's convenience."

DEaTH OF a SaLESMaN

The Internet makes it possible to render advertising more effective — through search engines that deliver customized ads. At Excite, a search for a word like "car" would lead to the delivery of a banner ad for Acura. Even more exciting is a development by a company called BlackSun: automated spokesmen. BlackSun developed the software for 3-D chat rooms in which visual cartoon-like characters interact. Into this arena they send ad robots for participating companies, designed to appear when chat room participants use specific words. It's called "immersive advertising." Just drop the word "clean" into your discussion and ad robot Dusty the Dustbuster will invite you for a private chat about his favorite vacuum cleaner. Not only can you program the robot's dialogue, said BlackSun in a delightful word combination, "you can program a robot's humanness."

Meanwhile, the tracking service for advertisers at *The New York Times'* website received a glowing review. Ami Goodhart, media director for K2 Design, said in an enthusiastic testimonial, "with *The New York Times'* registered data base, we were able to target the banners and know 100% that they were reaching the correct people." You can just imagine the relief they must have felt knowing that "incorrect" people weren't accidentally reading their promotions. Net Perceptions claimed their personalization tool "works like your company's best sales reps," getting to know customers on a one-to-one basis. Each time a customer returns, the program keeps learning and pools the knowledge "to broaden and deepen each relationship." Not only do customers benefit from having such "deep" relations, they won't even have to know they are having them. According to Ken Cassar of Jupiter Communication, "Customers won't notice it [the personalized tracking], but it will improve their shopping experience." What more could shoppers want?

Turn In Your Parents Dept.

Commercial websites for children are providing great opportunities for kids to participate and feel a sense of accomplishment by contributing valuable information about themselves. At the Mr. Jelly Belly site, for example, kids can earn candy by supplying information on their age, gender, address, and shopping habits. At the beginning of many online games, companies show their interest in each and every child by asking the above questions plus inquiring about their parents and grandparents. Sort of creates a family-corporate bond. But the best site has to be that of Mars Candy, which has a fun game called Impostor Search, where kids can help find fake M&M candy. The Junior Detectives just need to supply the names and e-mail addresses of their little friends and Mars would send out wanted posters to them while building up a modest database. M&M spokesperson Marilyn Machute countered criticism of Impostor Search by saying that the alerting of friends is just "part of the fun." Since it is fun, why do we have to think critically about it?

CHILD Protection report card

Ever wonder how all those surfwatch-type programs to protect our children on the Net have been doing? Several studies have show they are carrying out their jobs — and more. For example, a popular screening program called Cyber Patrol protects our young not only from pornography but also from the poetry of Anne Sexton. Quite a bonus. And for reasons only a sophisticated computer program could fathom, it also blocks out references to Sri Lanka. Net Nanny performs not nearly as well, allowing *Hustler* magazine's nature appreciation photos to come through. But it does successfully block out the "erotic" discussion of needlework. Censored are the sentences "Are there male parts to cross-stitch also, like I'd bother to waste my time!" and "Where exactly would you hang this in your house once you stitched it???" The best performer is called Cybersitter. It successfully blocks references to "homosexual," "gay rights," "NOW," "fascism," and "drugs." Best of all, it even blocks the site of a student activist group called Peacefire that has been critical of Cybersitter.

GOING BEYOND Mere Privacy

Do you wonder where all that information you give on questionnaires goes? It turns out much of it has been going to the Texas prison system, where inmates have been entering data on our personal lives for Metromail Corporation, a seller of direct marketing information. This fact was exposed after an Ohio woman named Beverly Denis started receiving e-mails from a stranger who knew all about her from entering data into her consumer file at Metromail. That 25-page file even contained information on how often she used room deodorizers, sleeping aids, and hemorrhoid remedies. Thanks to scanners and bar codes, marketing companies can track our purchasing history for individual products with precision. Naturally this has brought criticism. But defenders of surveillance like Chet Dalzell of the Direct Marketing Association point out that it's "beneficial to the whole economy, it's beneficial to consumers. It's just the marketplace trying to be intelligent." Do you really want a retarded marketplace? Don't we want to encourage markets that are at least trying to better themselves? Please spy on me! Meanwhile Robert Posch Jr., a VP for Doubleday, puts down the issue as "the ultimate touchy-feely issue." Privacy, he says, is just "some notion of the right to be left alone. Spare me."

employee recognition

A survey of 900 corporations by the American Management Association found that employers were taking a keen interest in the work of their employees. In fact, 67% of the firms were so interested in their workers that they practiced surveillance. The most widespread practice was monitoring phone calls, practiced by 37% of the firms. Growing in popularity were the practices of videotaping employees at work (16%) and reading e-mail and computer files (15%). Many companies (23%) assisted their workers by not informing them of the surveillance, thus not adding to their information overload. Critics of these management tools said they amounted to spying. But this is a simple misunderstanding according to Eric Greenberg, author of the AMA study, who "bristled" at the use of the term "spying." "The focus here is on security and employee performance," Greenberg said, "not on spying." He suggested the term "monitoring" be used instead. Or you may prefer Bellsouth Corp.'s more delicate "observations." There is a certain level of decorum that needs to be maintained here, after all.

privatizing big brother

More and more corporations have learned the value of customer surveillance. Harrah's Entertainment unveiled a giant databank that tracks the buying and gambling habits of six million of their customers. Their computers can now tell hotel clerks what you eat in their restaurants, what sweatshirts you buy in their giftshops, how much you spend on slot machines, and even what kind of mortgage you carry. This valuable information, much of it bought from credit card companies, is provided, said *The Wall Street Journal*, because it "helps clerks decide how to treat [customers] based on how much they are likely to lose." Why waste a valuable "hello"? Besides all the financial information, Harrah's computers also contain "emotional data" indicating whether you had a good time. And just how personal does their information get? According to Harrah VP Reg Mallama that it "depends on how valuable to me as a customer you are." It would be so embarrassing if there were nothing in your file.

New, Improved Freedom of Speech

Many of you are undoubtedly glad there are laws on the books keeping phone companies from handing out detailed information on who you call, all without your permission. How shortsighted, even selfish, this perspective can be was finally shown by the U.S. Court of Appeals (10th Circuit). In a landmark decision, the court ruled that such laws overlooked the First Amendment rights to free speech of struggling companies like US West, Sprint, MCI Worldwide, and Bell South. In the words of the court, "Although we may feel uncomfortable knowing our personal information is circulating in the world, we live in an open society, where information may pass freely." And mere discomfort should never outweigh fundamental rights. Next time you are placed under surveillance, remember the rights of those watching you. I love you, Big Brother.

Return of Air Safety

Back in 1997, long before Osama Bin Laden gained notoriety, airlines began "profiling" travelers using computers to track down potential terrorists. Critics worried the "profiles" might take on a racial flavor. Fortunately, as David Fuscus, a spokesman for the Air

Transport Association, says, the system does not discriminate against anyone because of their Muslim religion or Arab nationality. It just singles out travelers who have been going to countries with Muslim religions or those who have an Arab nationality, an important difference. In a major endorsement for computers, Fuscus adds, "There is no way the system operates that it could discriminate against people." But our ATA spokesman saves his clincher argument for last, noting that "the system had been approved by the Justice Department." Upon hearing this, the ACLU reportedly cast aside its objections, folded camp, and crept off into the desert.

"SMILE, YOU'RE ON CANDID CAMERA"

Not only corporations, but local governments have been discovering the benefits of electronic surveillance through remote-controlled camera networks. Whole cities can now be viewed block by block by hundreds of strategically placed cameras feeding video images into a central control room. The Port of New York and New Jersey has taken the lead in this exciting field with a grand total of 1,200 cameras monitoring its bridges and airports. Private companies are springing up to fill the need for complete video surveillance by police and TV stations. In New York, a video controller for the privately controlled Metro Networks is quoted as saying, "Rule of thumb, if you can see the Empire State Building, we can see you." Fortunately, there is an important safeguard protecting citizens' privacy. Says Kevin O'Reilly, operations manager for Shadow Traffic Network, "But really, we don't have a lot of time to look at people's apartments." That's a safeguard you can bank on.

FEELING NAKED

Citizens of Maryland may have woken up to a creative way their state Motor Vehicle Department has been raising funds. The MVD had been selling their computerized database of personal information to anyone with the money to access it. Now with only a computer and the aid of an "information broker" like CDB Infotek of Santa Ana, California, anyone can, for a fee, peruse any

Maryland resident's age, weight, driving record, unlisted phone numbers, property deeds, court cases, and medical conditions. Information brokers can give you access to public data from 48 states, although most are not as complete as those Maryland provides. Is this Big Brother at work? No, says Robert Mayer, chief information officer for the state of Maine. With electronic databases, "public records have become truly public." Especially for the "public" that can afford it.

SPeCIaL aGeNTS DePT.

New Jersey state troopers have been involving employees of dozens of hotels in the never-ending job of surveilling potential drug smugglers. State law enforcement officials have recruited hotel workers and trained them in special surveillance seminars to be informers on people who fit the profile of drug smugglers. What counts as suspicious behavior? The following: paying for rooms in cash, receiving too many phone calls, asking for corner rooms, and speaking in Spanish (a dead giveaway). Hotel managers have been routinely allowing state troopers to check through credit card receipts. Though some may view these actions as invasions of First Amendment rights, Fred Hartman, manager of a Newark Ramada Inn had a strong defense to offer. "They're good guys," he said, referring to the troopers, "and we want to cooperate with them whenever we can."

POLICe STaTe LITe

Orlando, Florida, followed the example of cities like Baltimore and installed surveillance cameras in downtown areas to help fight crime. This of course spurred a hot debate with the usual card-carrying ACLU types, who point to the possibilities of an Orwellian state. So as a public service, here are two rebuttals by Orlando civic leaders. First, Tim Holcomb, manager of Sir Speedy Printing, presented this argument: "The cops can't be on every corner. This is using technology to our benefit." And having police on every street is, of course, a goal we all share. Then there is Nigel Bassett, manager of Incredible Ink, who displayed his literary pedigree when he stated that the "only people who aren't going to like it are people who have something to hide" — like their copies of the Bill of Rights.

Helpful Hints

As surveillance becomes more pervasive, it becomes more difficult to communicate the strangeness of this intrusion into our private lives. One way of addressing this issue has been attempted by a theater ensemble in New York called The Surveillance Camera Players. These public-spirited citizens noticed that few people had thought of the welfare of security officers who must sit for hours behind the scenes watching boring television monitors. Believing that "a bored surveillant is an inattentive surveillant," The Surveillance Camera Players decided to put on plays "for the entertainment, amusement, and moral edification of the surveilling members of the law enforcement community." This sounds very much like the USO shows for the troops in World War II. The theatre group even posted a website explaining how you can put on your own plays. They recommend using pantomimes and making sure to have leaflets to explain your theater to customers. You may find their "10 Easy-to-Follow Steps!" to staging your own theatre presentation at http://www.notbored.org/the-scp.html. This may be a bit subtle as protest, but it does win a lot of style points.

Green-wash

greenwash, verb: to implement token environmentally friendly initiatives as a way of hiding or deflecting criticism about existing environmentally destructive practices

The decision by industry to "join forces" with environmentalists launched the genre of greenwash, which, despite the harsh definition above, has been a showcase of modern public relations. Ever since Weyerhauser became "the tree-growing company," I've quit agonizing over the fate of the wilderness. Among my favorite corporate slogans is that used by Mitsubishi for their wooden chopsticks in Japan: "Chopsticks that protect nature." Can't you just envision them standing guard over a forest — make that a forest about to be chopped down to make even more chopsticks. I must admit, the environmentalism of many companies has left me feeling guilty about not measuring up to their standards. For example, when Ford asked, "Shouldn't something built to take you where the air is fresh leave some fresh air for the rest of us?" I had to hide my head in shame. Of course, it was an ad for an SUV.

Not to be ignored, the government, too, has been making important contributions to this exciting field. But since 9-11, many issues, like oil drilling in Alaska's Arctic Wildlife Preserve, have had to be switched to the "national security" washing machine.

GOING GREEN MADE SIMPLE

Citizens for a Sound Economy, a free-market advocacy group, produced a model "Communications Guide" for Republicans and businesses that want to talk to the public about their commitment to preserving nature. Rule No. 1: "Focus groups show that people are more likely to empathize with your approach to environmental issues if they believe you are 'on their side'." (Thus Weyerhauser became "the tree-growing company.") The Guide suggests giving reasons for why you too want a good environment, such as having children, being an outdoor photographer, or simply enjoying the beauty of nature. Lastly, CSE tells its audience not to use the word reform. "Focus groups indicate people are more likely to respond positively to change when the word *modernizing* is used in describing our efforts on environmental protection." I must admit my delight in discovering that private property rights groups engage in "efforts on environmental protection." We're all for the environment now, it's just that developers and oil companies have a different way of expressing their environmental concerns.

NUCLEAR POWER GOES CLEAN

A while ago, ads touting the virtues of nuclear power showed up in some of our finer magazines (like *The New Republic*). Many of you may know already that nuclear reactors are "consistently safe," "proven economical," and "reliable." But those of you who can't spell "Chernobyl" may not be aware of how "environmentally clean" nuclear fission really is. And why is it so clean? Because, as the full-page color ad informs us, "Nuclear power plants don't burn anything to produce electricity, so they don't pollute the air." But there's more. Nuclear power plants produce "no greenhouse gas emissions, so they help protect the environment." Therefore they are environmentally clean, thanks to the fact that nuclear radiation has somehow ceased to count as a form of pollution. This news should relieve the minds of Hanford residents after reports of irradiated ants and tumbleweed in their backyards.

Three years later, the industry's message was being conveyed by the picture of an attractive young woman on a bicycle, talking into her cell phone, under the heading "Clean air is sooo 21st century." Just like radioactivity.

Tree HUGGING DePT.

A new environmental organization has moved to the forefront of groups trying to educate the public about global warming. The Greening Earth Society boasts one of the better environmental mottoes: "Humankind is a part of nature, rather than apart from nature." But while most groups stay fixated on the negative consequences of global warming like flooding and disease, The Greening Earth Society has chosen to focus attention on the "positive aspects of a rising level of carbon dioxide," and it does so in the belief that "nature is growing stronger, bigger, greener, and more resilient as a result of what we humans are doing to promote our own growth." The GES has special access to all the latest information because it shares offices and officers with the Western Fuel Association. (And who should know more about global warming than coal producers?) That's why they understand that using fossil fuels is "as natural as breathing." (That is, if you still can breathe.)

almost-environmental activism

The aluminum industry has taken the lead in efforts to save Columbia River salmon, joining with major utility companies to form Northwesterners for More Fish. But unlike other blind zealots for more fish, Alcoa and their friends have wanted to pursue the most "cost-effective" paths. At a meeting sponsored by Sen. Slade Gorton in Spokane, Washington, the new group announced plans to spend $800,000 educating Northwesterners on the need to use cost-benefit analyses to decide just how much "more fish" is enough and whether "each and every run of salmon" really needs to be saved. Interestingly, the fish used as a logo for the Northwesterners group turned out to be a carp, native to the East Coast, according to local fishermen. But then, NFMF never said exactly where they wanted more fish, did they?

Grass-roots Fertilizers

Among PR firms, APCO Associates, a pioneer in engineering perceptions for corporate clients in the political arena deserves special recognition. On their fine website, APCO describes for prospective customers a successful campaign in which they built grass roots coalitions to pass legislation on a "complicated issue" for a large trade association. APCO successfully "implemented grass-roots programs" (love that phrase), identified and trained "credible spokespersons," "assisted" in the writing of letters to newspapers and legislators, and even coordinated phone calls into radio talk shows. Thanks to the Internet, APCO is now openly sharing their accomplishments in purchasing grass-roots participation. In particular, it's reassuring to know that many of the letters on newspaper editorial pages have had professional "assistance." I'm sure that makes for an enriched reading experience.

Vanishing Acts

When the Bush Jr. team took office, the Fish and Wildlife Service faced a small dilemma with the content of their Arctic National Wildlife Refuge website, which was chockful of information showing how disastrous oil drilling would be to wildlife. Fortunately, they were able to separate the purely scientific information from mere interpretations of the data. For example, a summary of a Fish and Wildlife Service study (1987) on the impact of oil drilling on wildlife simply vanished. Also "disappeared" were sentences critical of oil drilling like the following: "Increased freezing depths of rivers and lakes as a result of water extraction (for ice road and pad construction and for oil well re-injection), have been killing overwintering [sic] fish and aquatic invertebrates." Other sections were "improved," like their description of the need for a network of roads through the wildlife refuge, which changed from "would" be required to a more diplomatic "may likely" be required. This advance in "objectivity" was discovered by an organization called Defenders of Wildlife.

CLearing THe waters

The Environmental Protection Agency has made significant improvements in a brochure on pesticides they have distributed nationally, thanks to help from food and pesticide industry lobbyists. For example, the old version presented "Tips to Reduce Pesticides on Foods," which the new version amended to "Healthy Sensible Food Practices." The old version suggested consumers consider buying food labeled "certified organic" while the improved version suggests the grocer "may be able to provide you with information about the availability of food grown using fewer or no pesticides." And where the old version listed actual health problems caused by pesticides, like birth defects, cancer, and nerve damage, the RSV simplifies it all as "health problems at certain levels of exposure." Much clearer, thanks to yet another example of successful cooperation between government and industry.

Defending our inner cities

For years, minority neighborhoods complained of having an unfair share of incinerators and garbage dumps placed in their areas. So the Environmental Protection Agency responded with regulations that forbade unfairly burdening racial minorities with sources of pollution. Fortunately, the U.S. Chamber of Commerce was looking out for their real interests. William L. Kovacs, the Chamber's VP, attacked such rules because they run "contrary to federal programs designed to bring jobs and cleanup to low-income and minority areas ..." Then he added, "No one is looking at the long-term economic benefit." (Of polluting, I believe he intended to say.) But Donald Welch, deputy secretary of the Pennsylvania Department. of Environmental Protection, topped him by arguing the EPA's actions were "disconnected from the real world of permit decision-making." That's the real world, for those of you who have been wondering.

"Organic" Gets a Face Lift

Hats off to the U.S. Agriculture Department for withstanding the attacks of wild-eyed extremists and stepping in to answer the question "What is organic food?" Thanks to their creative efforts, food that is irradiated, genetically engineered, or raised on municipal sewer sludge (American sewer sludge, I might add) can now proudly bear the label "organically grown." Despite the presence of metals and toxic substances in what is more politely termed "biosolids," none other than the Environmental Protection Agency defended their inclusion in the definition of "organic" because they are "more natural than commercially produced fertilizer." But it was in the fine print where our agriculture department really shone, eliminating a whole slew of extraneous labels that were just adding complications. These include the terms "produced without synthetic pesticides," "pesticide-free farm," "humanely-raised," "ecologically produced," and "no drugs or growth hormones used." Better to have just one label, don't you think?

Off to the Glue Factory

Back in 1971, Congress passed what seemed to be a pretty straightforward law to protect the tens of thousands of wild horses still roaming our plains. The Wild Free-Roaming Horses and Burros Act declared that it is "the policy of Congress that wild free-roaming horses and burros shall be protected from capture, branding, harassment or death." But then lawyers from the Department of the Interior arrived to clarify some of the provisions, thus freeing the law to be used to legitimate the slaughter of thousands of the wild horses. This modest reinterpretation came about when the government, in an act of mercy, began allowing ranchers to adopt horses from overcrowded grazing land. But then the Department of the Interior ruled that once the animals are adopted, "they are no longer 'wild' and the law says its criminal penalties only apply to 'wild' horses." Completely logical. So the horses can then be sold to the slaughterhouses, which is exactly what the government allows the ranchers to do after an "adoption."

NEW SPIN ON TREES

For many years, the timber industry had a hard time selling salvage logging on federal lands to the Congress. But what to call it? Representatives Helen Chenowith and Bob Schaeffer, both from Colorado, finally found an answer: Community Protection and Hazardous Fuels Reduction Act. Amongst the uncultured, the "hazardous fuels" to be reduced by this Act are known more commonly as "trees." More specifically, the Act is aimed at culling "predominantly" dying timber. But the best part is again in the fine print where we discover the depth of the timber industry's concern for the environment in these words: "Because of the strong concern for the safety of human life and property, and the protection of water quality, air quality and wildlife habitat, a sale ... shall not be precluded because the costs of the sale may exceed the revenue derived by the sale." Looks like you gotta go to a Weyerhauser lobbyist to find genuine environmentalism.

FAIRNESS FOR LOGGING COMPANIES

Environmental groups adopted a tactic of bidding on federal timberlands to preserve old-growth trees from rampaging chainsaws. Clever strategy, you say? Completely legal? Wrong, according to an "unauthorized" letter from agriculture undersecretary James Lyons denying the acceptability of "non-harvesting bids." The draft letter with Lyons' signature pointed out two devastating flaws barring the non-logging of public forest tracts. First, it costs money to produce environmental impact statements on logging. The letter points out that it "would be a wasteful use of public monies and contrary to the public interest" to produce reports on logging impacts and then sell the land to non-loggers. (Think of the bureaucrats whose feelings would be hurt over their wasted time.) Secondly, we might be encouraging unfair competition because "non-harvesting bidders would have few, if any, operating or personnel costs ..." Hardly fair to send Weyerhauser up against the economic clout of Earth First.)

ENDING POLLUTION

The state of Washington discovered an innovative way to stem the tide of dairy manures being dumped into its rivers. Under Senate Bill 6161, the phrase "dairy manure" was deleted in state laws and replaced with the more positive "dairy nutrients." The Dairy Nutrient Management Bill defined "dairy nutrient" as "any organic waste produced by dairy cows or a dairy farm operation." Sheryl Hutchinson, a spokeswoman for the state's Department of Ecology, said, "What they're trying to do is change dairymen's attitudes to view this dairy waste as a commodity." What Ms. Hutchinson did not explain was for whom chicken manure would suddenly become a nutrient. Despite the name change, I have no plans as yet to add it to my cereal. A footnote: the bill passed the state House by a vote of 97 to 1, with the lone dissenting vote coming from a former septic tank installer.

Helpful Hints

There is nothing quite like a gift given from the heart. For example, the organization Corporate Watch, which issues the annual Greenwash Awards, has also tried to reach out to potentially socially responsible CEOs with appropriate presents. Ford president William Clay Ford Jr. was awarded a recycled bicycle for commuting to work following his admission that SUVs did indeed pollute more than smaller cars. Unocal CEO Roger Beech was sent a "Made In Burma" backpack, the same type used by their "drafted" porters to carry heavy loads of military supplies in Burma. World Bank president James Wolfensohn was presented with scuba gear so he could visit indigenous villages submerged as a result of dams built with the help of the World Bank's "socially responsible investments." So far, I haven't heard whether thank-you notes have been received. Keep up with the fun at http://www.corpwatch.org.

Astroturf Politics

OVER 150,000 HIGHLY educated professionals are hard at work in the noble profession of managing public perceptions. Leading PR firms like Burson-Marsteller, Shandwick, Hill & Knowlton, and Edelman PR Worldwide are openly touting their skills, on their websites, in controlling public attitudes and orchestrating "grass-roots" support (with bogus "Letters to the Editor") for any lucrative cause. Corporate special interests have earned recognition for simplifying the job of politicians by allowing them to become full-time fundraisers while the remaining custodial duties of running the country are left to an assortment of twenty-two-year-old staff members. A final piece of information to file away: if Dante's vision of the Inferno is correct, all of them will be spending eternity burning in the eighth ring of Hell. Let us pray.

"ask NOT WHaT YOUr COUNTRY CaN DO FOr YOU ..."

Many citizens have a poor image of lobbyists. But the renewed willingness of lobbyists to serve their country after September 11th should help us see them in a truer light. To take just one example, Kenneth J. Kies, one of Washington's top corporate lobbyists, declared it would have been not only irresponsible but also unpatriotic for him to have refrained from seeking repeal of the corporate minimum income tax. This repeal would be worth about $20 billion to corporations specializing in overseas investments. "I wouldn't be doing the job," he said, "not necessarily for my clients — but for my country, if I wasn't being helpful in terms of offering ideas that can be helpful in stimulating the economy." His patriotic ideas: $1.4 billion for IBM, $832 million for General Motors ... Let's hear it for our lobbyists.

FASHION STATEMENTS

One reason many of us fail to participate in political events is that we don't know how to dress for the occasion. That's why it was so refreshing to see the National Association of Manufacturers come out with a memo to lobbyists detailing how they should dress for a political rally in support of President Bush's tax cut plans. To my complete surprise, the NAM recommended that lobbyists "dress down." The memo cautioned that "they do not need people in suits. If people want to participate — AND WE DO NEED BODIES — they must be DRESSED DOWN, appear to be REAL WORKER types, etc. We plan to have hard hats for people to wear. Other groups are providing waiters/waitresses, and other types of workers."

I mention this memo only because I believe there is a wonderful opportunity here for eager entrepreneurs to supply "real worker" outfits to business executives. Try picturing your favorite lobbyist in a rugged cowboy suit or a fireman's jacket with a plastic hatchet or a French maid's costume.

EXPORTING DEMOCRACY

Time magazine revealed in an exclusive behind-the-scenes article how American political consultants "secretly engineered" Boris Yeltsin's reelection in Russia. Campaign managers from California Governor Pete Wilson's election staff flew in disguised as TV salesmen and imported all the latest campaign techniques from polling to focus groups and "perception analyzers" to forge the victory. They even taught the Russians how to "go negative." They did just the type of job the CIA would have handled (or bungled) in the good old days. But after six pages describing the secrecy, intrigue, and image manipulation, what lesson did *Time* learn from this? As they gleefully trumpeted, "Democracy triumphed." Just like they teach it in high school civics.

SUPPOrT FOr POLITICAL ParTICIPATION

Bills to restrict soft money have met untimely deaths due solely, I believe, to the strength of the arguments mustered against them. The most brilliant attack against the campaign reform measure came from Sen. Mitch McConnel (R-Ky). He labeled it "an unconstitutional abrogation of the public's right to participate in the democratic process." So true. Shouldn't all of the public have the right to "participate" with hundred-thousand-dollar donations? Peggy Carter of RJR Nabisco, which donated $831,053, certainly thinks so. She defends these modest contributions as "an ageless part of the democratic process in this country" that "just allows us to get our toe in the door." Sadly, Ms. Carter had no words of wisdom on how those without $831,053 to donate can participate. What happens to their toes is unknown.

It turns out that those of you who are critical of politicians pandering to special interests for a steady diet of campaign payoffs could be suffering from "elitism." At least that's what Sen. Pat Roberts (R) from Kansas believes. "What a condescending, elitist point of view," he argued on the floor of the Senate, "that we should be free of asking people for their trust and support, their investment in good government, their partnership in good faith ..." Sobering words for unreflective elitists. But as you can see, the good senator was on a rhetorical roll, which culminated in this rather inspired reinterpretation of the "American way." Noting that we have a number of filters through which candidates must be sifted, Sen. Roberts asked, "Is a candidate's ability to attract campaign funds any less important to this process than his or her ability to attract votes?" Certainly not. It's right there in the Constitution, isn't it? Okay, so it isn't. But in all fairness, maybe we should decide elections on the basis of both votes and fundraising, giving points for each — just like in figure skating.

IT Never Happened Here

If you've worried about illegal campaign activity in the White House, rest easy. It never happened. Attorney General Janet Reno and her crack staff at the Justice Department revealed that no illegal campaign contributions were "solicited" or "received" by Al Gore, Maggie Williams (the First Lady's chief of staff), or any other administration official. First, no money was even "contributed" because "the definition of 'contribution' does not include soft money." In addition, the money that was not contributed, like the $50,000 handed Ms. Williams, was not "received." Why was it not received, those of you without benefit of three years of legal education ask? According to *The Washington Post*, because people like Williams, by White House reasoning, could not "technically 'receive' campaign contributions because they are not officers of a political party or campaign. Therefore the law prohibits something, that by this argument, cannot even occur." Now is that cutting-edge or not?

Dinner Prices in Washington, D.C.

The Clinton administration left the Republicans with an easy-to-follow price list for social gatherings. According to leaked documents, for a $10,000 to $25,000 donation you could buy an intimate dinner with the Vice-President or a dinner with the President and 100 of his friends. For only $50,000 you could have a private dinner with Bill and talk about how America has become, in his words, "hostage" to moneyed interests. CEO William Brandt explained it best after hosting a $10,000-a-plate dinner for the President at his home in Chicago. He and his guests, he said, just wanted to send a message: "End of story. It's American participatory democracy." Just like in the textbooks. Lorraine Voles, spokeswoman for Al Gore, had some helpful tips on how we should address these "participants." Speaking of the guests at Gore's thank-you party for his 200 largest contributors, Ms. Voles said, "You call them donors. They call themselves friends of the Vice-President." Did y'all catch that distinction?

Why are business leaders willing to pay $10,000 or more to eat with our nation's leaders? In the words of one CEO, Sean O'Keefe of Los Angeles, "To the rest of America this may sound ridiculous, but $10,000 is a small amount to pay to converse with intelligent people that will be able to help you." Well, Sean, have I got a deal for you at only half the price. Give me a call.

MOM AND APPLE PIE DEPT.

Republican leaders met in a weekend retreat in Palm Beach, Florida, with members of "Team 100", the elite club for donors who've written $100,000 checks for the GOP. Defending the right of party supporters to make such generous contributions was Senate majority leader Trent Lott, who declared, "I think for them to have the opportunity to do that is the American way." After waving a tiny flag, Lott put forth a horrifying vision of what could happen without the efforts of wealthy corporate donors, affirming that Republicans are "not for food stamps for politicians." Not to worry, with friends like these. Republican spokeswoman Mary Crawford countered criticism that the retreat was about the rich buying access by saying she "would go anywhere in the country to get together with 200 people who have a real commitment to building the party." Meanwhile a Republican fundraising letter surfaced that promised "an unprecedented level of dialogue with House Republicans and party leaders" for a paltry $15,000, which, I must say, was not as good a deal as the Democrats' bargain basement price of $10,000.

INVESTING IN AMERICA

A study on the returns special interests are getting for their investments in politicians was released by the Center for Responsive Politics. To everyone's total surprise, the Center found a direct correlation between money donated to legislators and their votes on issues. For example, when environmentalists tried to repeal the salvage law that allowed timber companies a free hand in cutting old-growth trees, the vote failed 54 to 42. Senators siding with the timber industry averaged $19,503 in timber PAC contributions while those opposed averaged a mere $2,675. It all sounds very damning until you hear the rest of the story as told by the special interests themselves. Chris West of the Northwest Forestry Association explained their $71,230 investment in Senator Slade Gorton was a result of their agreement with him on a broad range of issues. In a statement as dense as the fir trees they clearcut, West said, "They're not buying his vote on one bill" No, they buy it for a lot of bills. It's cheaper by the dozen.

ENDOWMENTS FOR DEMOCRACY

The outcry over China funneling money to the Democrats in the '96 election finally jogged a reporter's memory about the U.S. engaging in the same practice. John Broder reported in *The New York Times* that Congress routinely appropriates $30 million a year for the National Endowment for Democracy. The NED spends those funds on candidates and "institution building" in countries like Nicaragua, Portugal, North Ireland, Bolivia, and China (which had received $1.6 million the previous year). However, Louisa Coan, NED's program officer for East Asia, was quick to point out that their spending in elections in foreign countries is not comparable to other nations meddling in our affairs. The difference? Here is Louisa Coan again: "We support people who otherwise would not have a voice in their political system ... where governments or other social forces prevent open and peaceful political processes." I should point out that she was not referring to our country. Which brings us to our contest. See if you can guess where the NED's program officer was hiding during the revelations about the $10,000 donations needed just to gain access to our officials.

STEALTH CAMPAIGN

The inside accounts of "The Selling of the President 1996" leaked out and one of the juiciest stories is how Clinton campaign organizers Dick Morris and Bill Knapp cleverly fooled the press. Early in the campaign, polling results showed that there was an effective way to shift the terms of debate by making a preemptive strike on the Republicans on the Medicare issue. Knapp and Morris first had Clinton watch old Reagan videos to develop that "air" of command and then filmed ads with him meeting the public under the slogan "Doing what's moral, good, and right by our elderly." But for this campaign to work, they knew it had to be conducted secretly so the press wouldn't alert the Republicans and allow them time to counterattack. But how could they reach millions of swing voters without awakening the ever-vigilant press corps? Bill Knapp came up with the answer. They kept it secret by spending millions advertising all over the country, but not advertising in the New York, Los Angeles, or Washington, D.C., markets. Nor did they issue any press releases about it. The strategy worked. Two thousand "investigative" reporters covering the campaign missed the story, Bill's numbers went up, and everybody lived happily ever after.

FELLOWSHIP IN HIGH PLACES

For those who've worried that national politicians have been skimming all the corporate payoffs, there's good news. A select group of 100 corporations has been giving millions to the National Governors' Association. These corporate "fellows," as they are called, include firms like AT&T, Exxon, General Motors, Dow, and Phillip Morris. In return for their largesse, they receive special briefings, their own work and meeting space at annual conventions, and the opportunity to help shape policy in staff meetings. According to an NGA fact sheet, this allows executives to "become better acquainted with governors' staffs and to share common interests." Like backgammon and stamp collecting, I presume. The Governors' group defended this practice as being perfectly legal and "aimed only at getting the best advice on important issues."

What ogres would want to deprive our governors of the wisest counsel? NGA meetings are open to the public, although unfortunately, possibly due to a lack of publicity, only lobbyists have bothered to attend.

New Civil Rights

The Democratic National Committee decided to refuse injections of foreign campaign donations. This raised an outcry of discrimination from foreign-owned businesses in the U.S. Apparently the DNC spaced out and forgot how many companies are foreign-owned. A host of major corporations like Universal Studios, Seagram's Whiskey, and Brown & Williamson will now be barred from contributing to the Democrats because their owners lack green cards. Unfair? Yes, says Sidney Sheinberg, one of the Democrats' biggest contributors: "People should have the right in a democracy to give money." Then, in a classic statement, our budding protester added, "I'm not sure I understand the logic of it; influence is influence, whether it's foreign or domestic." So true. A buck is a buck and a bought-off senator is a bought-off senator. What's the problem in the age of globalization? Fortunately, there may be little need to worry, for as *The Wall Street Journal* told its readers, "fundraising records suggest it won't be hard to get around the rules." Now that's reassuring.

Welfare Slashing Made Simple

The Republicans published a 17-page guide on how to put a "positive spin" on their "get 'em back to work" welfare laws. The guide for GOP congressional types explains to them in "layman's terms" how to hold "Oprah style" town meetings to push success stories about people getting off welfare. For no extra money, politicians can also learn how to pose at press events with a "disabled child who will continue to receive benefits." The architect of the brilliant *Members' Guide to Explaining the New Welfare Law to Constituents* was Rep. E. Clay Shaw (R-Fl). With over 135,000 disabled children slated to lose benefits, Rep. Shaw was concerned about the "doomsday people" in the press who have been giving the reforms a negative spin. He notes that the scare stories about people losing benefits were "discouraging to people trying to get off welfare." Whether that is as discouraging as the lack of jobs paying above-poverty wages, he didn't say.

WHere's Forrest GUMP?

The Democratic National Committee has come out with its master plan for taking back the talk radio airwaves. The key instruction for candidates in the 11-page memo by Jon-Christopher Bua is, and I kid you not, to "sound dumb." The idea is for candidates to come on at first like Andy of Mayberry with their conservative talk show hosts and then "really unload" with facts and figures later in the interview. Sadly, instructions are not provided on how to sound dumb, not that all candidates would need it. Further tips from the memo: When a host tries to slam you with facts, "change the subject." And if a caller raises a hot topic, answer with "I understand that the President is a very religious man and is a regular churchgoer." Next we'll see DNC scouts out scouring our special ed classrooms looking for future candidates. (Although it looks like the Republican presidential scouts beat them to the punch.)

selling THe war ON Drugs

The Republican campaign for a drug-free America hit a bump when its PR script, with approved sound bites and visual props, was leaked. The one-page memo gave Republican leaders "communication ideas" and a handy list of descriptive adjectives to enliven their speeches. These included power words such as "epidemic," "scourge," and "poison;" props like needles and syringes; and ways to get Democrats to "buy into it." But even better was the Republican response to the disclosure of their behind-the-scenes media manipulations. An unnamed top congressional aide demonstrated a keen grasp of the issues when commenting, "That kind of stuff would be better off just talked about." Another Republican press secretary, Pete Jeffries, put it all in perspective when he defended the use of PR memos by leaders who "need to know what the event's all about so when they're in the spotlight they can perform." Like trained seals, I presume.

special interest watchers

A public interest group called Contributions Watch published a widely reported study on the massive campaign contributions of trial lawyers. Describing itself as a citizens' group dedicated to "full disclosure," CW set out to publicize cases where "a single special interest gives an enormous amount of money while remaining largely invisible ..." Unfortunately, CW neglected to mention at the time that they were almost totally funded by a lobbying firm of Phillip Morris. A modest oversight. Admitting its guilt, the tobacco front group declared, "Regardless of funding, the public record is still accurate." Good point. Who should understand better than Phillip Morris how small an influence money has on scientific results? And who better to be alert to invisible special interests lurking behind public causes?

"BUT everYBODY'S DOING IT"

In California, an organization called Californians for Telecommunications Choice has been attacking Pacific Bell for its monopolistic ways. Due to an oversight, I'm sure, CTC forgot to tell anyone that it was largely funded by AT&T for its campaign to get state legislators to open up the phone market to more competition, something AT&T has always supported (ahem). But AT&T spokeswoman Alice Nagle was ready with a stout defense of her company's practice. "All big corporations," she said, "are involved with coalitions, so it's a normal, ethical business decision to align" with CTC. I hope everyone caught this new meaning of the term *ethical*: it now describes what all big corporations do. You might want to pencil it into your *Webster's* Dictionary.

California was not the only state where this modern-day trust buster was carrying on the fight against monopoly control. Ma Bell had also been funding "grass-roots" organizations (while modestly not mentioning itself) that were opposed to the $56-billion merger of SBC Communications of San Antonio and Ameritech of Chicago. AT&T executive James Cicconi revealed the conglomerate's dream of the future: "AT&T's vision is one of more competition and more consumer choice at every level with open competition at the local level that doesn't now exist." Mr. Cicconi's words were punctuated by news that AT&T was pursuing a $32-billion acquisition of TCI's cable network. The result: more and more competition and consumer choice (ahem).

Helpful Hints

One of our more popular indoor sports is the building of parody websites. For example, James Baumgartner, a student in Troy, NY, decided he wanted to "evoke public commentary concerning an issue which is at the core of this nation's democracy: whether or not elections are for sale." So he created a website called www.voteauction.com, where people could supposedly buy and sell votes in the presidential election. The site was so realistic the Chicago Board of Election Commissioners sued to shut down the site and sent James a most nasty letter. James had to explain to them it was a parody.

In the old days, when people became angered at a company like Exxon, they would write a letter that was promptly ignored. Now in almost the same time, you can put up a simple website. Do be careful when listing your site with major search engines. If your site is called "Exxon Sucks," for example, many people will inadvertently pull it up when searching for "Exxon." The World Trade Organization ran into this problem when a parody WTO site was created (http:gatt.org). They even had to post a warning about the false site, describing it as a "nuisance for serious users looking for genuine information."

Bureau-Arthritis

"WE DON'T PRACTICE propaganda in this country ..." That announcement by Maj. Joe LaMarca, spokesman for the U.S. Central Command, while speaking about Iraq, pretty well let the air out of the tires of political satirists. With nothing left to do, I opted to do just "straight" reporting on the accomplishments of our federal government. They were many. Surprisingly, the much vaunted "downsizing" of federal agencies seemed to have little impact on the production of quality Newspeak. We still have the best money can buy. And a word for those of you expecting a pile of "Bushisms." This book is about cutting-edge *advances* in Newspeak and not about how far you can trip over your tongue. The man did not make it over this bar (and a few others).

ADVANCED FLAG-WAVING

The House of Representatives had the dubious honor of actually passing the Republican-sponsored Economic Security and Recovery Act, aimed at pumping $100 billion into the economy, most of it directed to corporations and the rich. The naked centerpiece of the stimulus bill was the repeal of the corporate minimum tax, a gift of $25 billion to corporations restrained from realizing the full benefits of their tax shelters, complete with rebates for taxes paid going back to 1986. Taxpayers would be handing IBM $1.4 billion, Ford $1.0 billion, General Motors $832 million — not for any new investments in America but for having invested their money outside our borders or in tax shelters.

But now comes the fun flag-waving part. How do you defend such pork? Fortunately, the House held a debate, so we can quote some of the finer rhetorical flourishes, and then I'll let you judge. First up to bat was Rep. John Linder (R-Ga), who pointed out on the House floor that we needed this measure to ensure our economic security "in light of the tragic events of September 11, 2001." That's $1.4 billion for IBM, $1.0 billion for Ford Motors, $832 million for General Motors ... as sort of a memorial to the victims, I presume. Rep. Kevin Brady (R-Tx) rose to proclaim that we "cannot stand by idly and let a terrorist topple our economy as they toppled the World Trade Center." Obvious conclusion: We need to give $671 million to General Electric, $608 million to Texas Utilities, $600 million to DaimlerChrysler ... Even more spirited was the response of Rep. James Traficant (R-Oh) who answered Democratic critics: "Let it go with this class warfare business. It hurts America. This is an important bill, as important as any we have dealt with that deals with terrorism. We are defeating terrorism." Defeating Bin Laden with cash handouts of $572 million to Chevron Texaco, $371 million to United Airlines ... I assume he's ready to surrender.

The high point of the debate came when the main sponsor of this bill, Rep. Bill Thomas (R-Ca), addressed the House. Rep. Thomas prefaced his remarks by saying, "Sometimes we actually run into problems when we are dealing with plain English." How true. Then he asked, "Does anyone dispute that making sure the economy remains strong so that we can be a vigilant and free America is combating terrorism?" Sounds like $254 million to Enron ... Rep. Thomas also had an answer for the negativity critics directed toward corporations. We mustn't lose sight of the fact, he said, that "businesses are America's employers. They're the hardware store, the diner down the street, the gas station on the corner." Take a wild guess how much the corner diner would be receiving. Meanwhile, where was I? Oh yeah, it's $241 million for Phillips Petroleum ...

"WHO'S ON FIRST ..."

The U.S. Department of Health and Human Services came in for serious criticism over its handling of the anthrax scare. It topped off a particularly poor PR week by offering reassurances to postal workers that they needn't take antibiotics, shortly before two of them died from the disease. Fortunately, Campbell Gardett, a spokesman for the agency, was able to find just the right spin to defend his agency's performance. "Something that's factual at this moment proves not to be factual in retrospect," he said. "That doesn't mean it wasn't factual at the time." Connoisseurs may want to compare this to the declaration of former press secretary Ron Ziegler during the Reagan years that a previous statement had become "inoperative." We could call this another exercise in "reinventing government."

CHIP OFF THE OLD BLOCK DEPT.

When George Bush, Jr. decided to push for a major tax cut in his presidential campaign, he had to take care not to make the kind of mistake his father made when he referred to a tax increase as a "revenue enhancement." His campaign also needed to correct a common misperception, that Bush's tax reform favored the rich. As Lawrence Lindsay, Bush's chief economic advisor, carefully explained, "We're not giving it to the wealthy, we're repairing problems in the tax code." Understand the difference? It's comprehending these fine distinctions that sets our government leaders apart.

NEW, IMPROVED GOVERNMENT

The Clinton administration may actually have left an important legacy in the exciting field of "reinventing government", according to a study by Paul C. Light of the Brookings Institute. While cutting a record 350,000 civil service jobs, they further "streamlined" government by adding 16 new administrative layers at the top, as many as created by the previous seven administrations combined. As a public service, I am going to clarify a few of these vital job titles. First among the new positions is the *deputy associate deputy secretary*, who should not be confused with the *associate deputy assistant secretary* or the *assistant deputy assistant secretary*, both of whom report to the *principal deputy assistant secretary* and not the *deputy associate assistant secretary*, as some mistakenly believe. The post of *associate assistant administrator* has been lost, but that role has been ably filled by the *deputy associate deputy administrator*, not to be confused with the *associate deputy assistant administrator* or, for that matter, the *assistant deputy administrator* who, as you will remember, works under the *associate deputy administrator*. Questions, anyone?

POLITICaL UPGraDe

A surprise announcement that we had been promoted beyond the status of mere democracy was made in Zaire, by Earl Young, the CEO of American Mineral Fields. Mr. Young and his mining company had been buying diamonds from both sides in Zaire's civil war. But was Mr. Young worried about what might happen if the leftist rebels won? No. In fact, he oozed with optimism during an NPR interview, secure in the knowledge that since we'd won the Cold War, people know that "capitalism is a good form of government." Those not afflicted with Alzheimer's may remember that capitalism was once viewed as a form of the economy while the government was something other than capitalism. At first, I chuckled at Mr. Young's words as the faux pas of a nouveau riche type unschooled in the subtleties of the country club. Then I was set straight by *The Wall Street Journal*. Reporting on the need for a counterintelligence czar to defend national and corporate secrets, the *Journal* noted, "With the rise in globalization and industrial espionage, government officials now say national security and economic security are indistinguishable." So there. "Capitalism is a good form of government" — I'll write it on the blackboard 100 times. Okay? Or, in the immortal words of John Jay, our nation's first Chief Justice, "The people who own the country ought to govern it."

"OF HUMAN BONDAGE"

Congress finally passed legislation banning the importation of goods made by indentured children. The bill, sponsored by Rep. Bernie Sanders, managed to pass in spite of the compassionate concerns of house republicans that, in the words of *The New York Times*, "it might be expensive for Customs to enforce it." U.S. purchases of rugs and soccer balls help maintain much of the estimated 15 million indentured children in Asia, so it was good news that we were finally able to afford to curtail our trade. Surprisingly, there had been a law on the books since 1930 banning the importing of goods made by indentured or convict labor "under penal sanctions." But customs officials, in one of their more memorable feats of bureaucratic hairsplitting, ruled the law did not apply to children because they did not work "under penal sanctions" as the law required. So for 67 years we have been abetting the enslavement of millions of children because these youngsters lacked the foresight to have been convicted of a crime before they became indentured workers.

"IF YOU CAN'T BE WITH THE ONE YOU LOVE ..."

In the wake of the Chinese spying scandal, the Department of Energy wasted no time in issuing new pages of regulations to tighten security in our nation's nuclear labs. The key provision makes for some great reading. Employees at nuclear sites will be required to report on any "close and continuous contact" with foreign citizens from a list of 25 nations. However, in a major concession, the DOE decided that one-night stands would be exempt from reporting requirements. Apparently they do not threaten national security as would a two-night affair. Rumor has it the Energy Department was concerned about overwhelming their staff with paperwork. And in a notable concession to reality, the DOE decided employees must report regardless of whether they know or remember their sexual partner's name. Thank God, the spirit of the sixties is still alive somewhere.

Foreign Service Goes Scientific

The U.S. Foreign Service works diligently to assure that only foreigners with proper intentions are issued visas to visit the U.S. To improve their performance, at least one office in Brazil has been using a very scientific coding system that was leaked to the press by a disgruntled employee who felt it reflected racial discrimination. Nit-picking aside, here are some of the sociological categories that foreigners fall into. First there are LP for "Looks Poor" and TP for "Talks Poor." Below these categories are LR for "Looks Rough" and TC for "Take Care" (I wouldn't even want to see these types). On the top end is RK for "Rich Kid." Pretty scientific. According to the State Department, these categories are "sensible tools" to weed out potential visa cheaters. U.S. Attorney Sherry Harris argued that even though these categories "may at first glance appear insensitive," there was nothing discriminatory about them. Just because they seem to target poor people, who in Brazil are overwhelmingly black, doesn't mean discrimination occurs. Obvious, isn't it?

The Full-Monty Rules

Only in America did the following regulation have to be written. For years the Occupational Safety and Health Administration has taken the reasonable step of requiring employers to provide toilets. One throne is required for up to 15 employees and two for the next 16 to 35 and so on. But OSHA committed a gross oversight in making their regulations. They forgot to explain why the toilets were needed. So in 1998 they had to make a new rule requiring employers to "make toilet facilities available so that employees can use them when they need to do so." Duh. Let's just hope the regulations require doors that open and close on the toilets. And toilet paper. And instructions on how to use the toilet paper safely.

The IRS Stands and Delivers

Back in 1985, a 93-year-old man absentmindedly sent a check for $7000 to the Internal Revenue Service. Several years after his death, his daughter, Marian Brockamp, discovered the overpayment and wrote to the IRS. Instead of a nice thank-you note and a check, the

IRS stuck to its regulations and refused to refund the money that had never been owed. The matter went to the U.S. Circuit Court where Ms. Brockamp won a decision. But then, the Justice Department stepped in on behalf of the IRS and announced it would appeal the decision to the Supreme Court. Why? Because, they argued, " the tax agency should not be forced to reopen thousands of old cases, regardless of the reason." And just how insane could this get, you ask? Listen to the initial response of the high court. Brockamp's attorney Frederick Daily recalls, "The very first question, from Justice Ruth Ginsburg was: 'What does your case have to recommend itself, other than fairness?'" He adds, "I knew I was in trouble at that point." Indeed, he was. Case closed.

COMING-OUT PARTY

Departing President Clinton, as a final gift to the nation, created the position of counterintelligence czar. Besides coordinating the efforts of countless agencies to defend national secrets, the czar has the added task of protecting critical secrets for American corporations. *The Wall Street Journal* reported that intelligence officials were hopeful they could find someone "having the stature to engage chief executives." But when corporations are keeping secrets from the public, should the government be acting as an accomplice? Well, yes. Why? As the *Journal* explained, in words WTO protesters should learn by heart, "With the rise in globalization and industrial espionage, government officials now say national security and economic security are indistinguishable." To update the words of revolutionary war hero Nathan Hale, "I regret I have but one life to give for my country ... and for Mobil Oil and Boeing and Time Warner and ..."

SETTING THE BAR HIGHER

Governors get so little recognition that we thought we'd honor Alabama's beloved Fob James, Jr. as our Model Newspeak Governor. Here's just a partial list of his accomplishments during one year:

1. He threatened to call out the National Guard to defend the display of the Ten Commandments in courts.
2. He reintroduced chain gangs.
3. He wrote a 34-page letter to the Supreme Court explaining why the Bill of Rights does not apply to states.
4. He put his staff to work trying to model the state government on the Waffle House restaurant chain.
5. He spent $3,000 of state money sending a book explaining creationism to biology teachers.
6. He advised teachers on how to give troublesome students "a pop on the fanny."
7. He explained to ministers the way to end violence: "A good butt-whipping and then a prayer is a wonderful remedy." George Wallace, not even in his prime, never had a year like Fob James, Jr.

Helpful Hints

Civil disobedience has had so much attention that people sometimes forget the benefits of civil obedience. Obeying the rules can be fulfilling, especially when you do it with a large group. Some years ago in San Antonio, Texas, a group of poor residents discovered local banks were redlining their neighborhood. Someone noticed that nobody had any dimes or nickels. So they all decided to visit a few of their local banks so they could make change. Everyone followed the rules and waited patiently in line. An "unexpected" consequence was that bank business was brought to a virtual standstill. A shame. I'm told some organizations have rules that, if followed to the letter, can result in very low productivity. So be careful. But do remember, if football fans can do the wave, you too can do fun things in unison.

Perma-War

L ET'S FACE IT, Osama Bin Ladn was a gift from heaven for the Bush administration. Our nation has trained for years for one job: being the world's policeman in the fight against Evil. That's all we know how to do. Eisenhower, Kennedy, Johnson, Nixon, that guy who stumbled all the time, Carter, and Reagan — all had the Evil Empire. Then came hard times as dad tried to make do with Saddam and Clinton had a leftover war on drugs. People actually questioned defense spending. Then Osama brought us a budget war that promises to go on for years and years, putting us back in the saddle. One of the major lessons of Orwell's *1984* is that you have to have an enemy. We're back to following the script.

WAR MARKETING

One of the hottest war planning issues was settled with the announcement that The Rendon Group had been chosen to help manage our public relations effort against the Taliban. The Rendon Group has served corporations and governments in 71 nations. Rendon is known, according to its website, for their "hands on approach" to managing crises, which have been well-tested in the Middle East. In Saudi Arabia, Rendon designed a traffic safety game show for Toyota that helped increase "loyalty to Toyota." Rendon not only performed "outreach" for the government of Kuwait, they also designed a "proactive communications program" for the Kuwait Petroleum Corporation when it was faced with the prospect of a labor strike.

In what may be unrelated news, it was announced that Wayne Newton would be sent overseas to entertain our troops. I'm told this news led to a 200% increase in the number of soldiers volunteering for front line duty and, inexplicably, a similar increase in the number of soldiers volunteering for solitary confinement.

PERCEPTION MANAGEMENT (RAMBO DIVISION)

Millions were excited when Secretary of State Colin Powell appointed Charlotte Beers, the "queen of Madison Avenue," to head our war's publicity campaign. This was only fitting for, as Powell explained, "We're selling. We're selling a product. That product we are selling is democracy. It's the free enterprise system, the American value system." Ms. Beers' ads for Head & Shoulders shampoo and Uncle Ben's Rice certainly demonstrated our war was in the right hands.

Unfortunately, my favorite group was overlooked in the process and I'd like to make a pitch for them. Behavior Modification Operation is, according to their website, a "unique international corporate advisory company ready to fulfill your specific behavior modification requirements." BMO has trained personnel with military and psychological warfare backgrounds ready to "facilitate local acceptance of your organization's objectives." What I particularly like is BMO's guarantee that your operations will be "sympathetically supported by both antagonistic and indifferent local population groups." No questions asked. No wimpy hand wringing about "human rights." That's a real man's organization.

ADVANCED FINGER POINTING

In the Desert War against Iraq, the phrase "collateral damage" would appear in news accounts with quotation marks. By the time of our bombing of Afghanistan, the quotation marks had been dropped. But photos of injured or dead Afghani children still presented a problem, unless your name was Donald Rumsfeld. As our Secretary of State explained, "When the Taliban issue accusations of civilian casualties, they indict themselves." Why? Because "their leadership are the ones that are hiding in mosques and using Afghan civilians as human shields by placing armor and artillery in close proximity to civilian schools and the like." They are, as another senior defense official put it, "inviting collateral damage." As it is a widely accepted practice in the West to machine-gun hostages in order to capture criminals hiding behind them, we can't be held up to blame.

eDUCaTIONaL aCHIeVeMeNTS

The School of the Americas, the U.S. military training center for respected Latin American military leaders, like El Salvador's Death Squad leader Roberto D'Aubuisson and Panama's Gen. Manuel Noreiga, has been subject to protests and constant criticism. In defending the school's reputation, U.S. spokesperson Maj. Gordon Martel stepped forward to report the other side of the story. "Out of 59,000 students," he proudly proclaimed, "less than 300 have been cited for human rights violations like torture and murder and less than 50 have been convicted of anything." Certainly a record any of our major universities could take pride in. But Major, try to think real hard. Could there possibly be a reason why so few have been cited or convicted? A reason besides good behavior? Think real hard and maybe it will come to you.

The School of the Americas came in for yet another round of criticism with the publication of portions of one of their training manuals, which urged the use of "fear, payment of bounties for enemy dead, beatings, false imprisonment, executions ..." I know it sounds bad, but wait before condemning this fine school. A Pentagon investigation found the use of the manual was the result of a "bureaucratic oversight." So rest easy. In fact, this training manual, used from 1982 to 1991, was found to be using "outdated instructional material without the required doctrinal approval." Just like our public schools. And it only took them nine years to correct the "oversights." Thank goodness we have an efficient military apparatus in place to catch "outdated" — as opposed to "morally offensive" — teachings.

The Baltimore Sun later unearthed a fine 1983 teaching manual used by the CIA for the edification of our Latin American neighbors. The title alone, *Human Resources Exploitation Manual*, would earn it a Newspeak honorable mention. The manual was used by the security forces of five Latin American countries in a three-week course that was followed by two weeks of "practical exercises" (and I don't want to know what those were). It seems, in comparison, quite tame, calling for the avoidance of physical torture in the interrogation of prisoners. Mental forms of torture like exhaustion and isolation of a prisoner were praised for "destroying his will to resist" (just like in Orwell's 1984). However, the manual adds an important qualification: "While we do not stress the use of coercive techniques, we do want to make you aware of them and the proper way to use them." In that same spirit, maybe they could have changed their title to *Human Resources Exploitation Awareness Manual*. Would have had more of a new-age feel to it, don't you think?

Price Quotes on Children

After the Gulf War, our blockade of Iraq led to the deaths of an estimated half a million young children from disease and malnutrition. CBS Reporter Lesley Stahl had a chance to interview our then soon-to-be Secretary of State Madeleine Albright about this sensitive issue. Asked Stahl: "We have heard that a half million children have died. I mean, that's more children than died in Hiroshima. And — and you know, is the price worth it?" to which Albright responded, "I think this is a very hard choice, but the price — we think the price is worth it." This answer has, of course, left open the question of exactly what price would not be "worth it": 500,001, 500,002, 500,003 ...? And with inflation? I'm betting that by the time you read this, the State Department will have figured out a precise figure. Go ask them, they have top quality people working there. Their e-mail address is AskPublicAffairs@state.gov.

CRIMINAL CONSPIRACIES DEPT.

Somewhere buried deep inside the U.S. Treasury Department sits the Office of Foreign Assets Control. This obscure department finally had its day in the sun when they discovered that members of the peace organization Voices in the Wilderness had violated the embargo against exporting goods to Iraq. (Apparently Voices had issued press releases announcing the fact, little suspecting the eagle-eyed OFAC agents would be on to them.) More specifically, Voices in the Wilderness was fined $120,000 for the "exportation of donated goods, including medical supplies and toys" to Iraq. Apparently these peace activists were unable to comprehend how our policy of banning toys for Iraqi children is bringing Saddam to his knees. Even more seriously, OFAC director R. Richard Newcomb cited the organization's leaders for forming "a conspiracy formed for the purpose of engaging in transactions prohibited by the Regulations." That's "Regulations" with a capital "R".

SELLING ARMS TO OUR FRIENDS

The Clinton administration finally ended the U.S. policy of not selling advanced weapons to Latin America. The U.S. has been loathe to set off local arms races between prestige-seeking dictators, but the current menu of stable democracies has brought changes in our thinking. In the words of Assistant Secretary of State Thomas McNamara, the U.S. had to allow Latin American countries to modernize their militaries "as any modern democracy would." Imagine a democracy without the latest stealth bomber? But the prize for best use of the English language in defense of enlarging the military porkbarrel for Lockheed goes to White House spokesperson Michael McMurry. Just listen to his scintillating prose: "It is in America's national security interest to promote stability and security among our neighbors in the hemisphere by engaging them as equal partners as they modernize and restructure their defense establishment." So let's order another round of F-16 fighter planes for our new found "equal partners." A final note: When Belarus went ahead and sold two types of advanced aircraft to Peru, Washington warned, according to *The*

New York Times, that "they threatened regional stability." Unlike our arms sales, of course.

THE real GULF War SYNDrOMe

After living in denial, the Pentagon finally admitted they had known since 1991 that U.S. troops had been exposed to chemical weapons in the Gulf War. This came in the wake of findings by a Presidential advisory committee that 1,100 soldiers had been exposed to nerve gas when an Iraqi ammunition dump was blown up. That committee also chastised the Defense Department for conducting a "superficial investigation" that had "gravely undermined" the credibility (!) of the Pentagon. But how do we explain the fact that officials knew as early as November 1991 of the chemical exposure while the department was officially denying it? A Pentagon official, apparently with a very straight face, blamed it on "gross clerical errors." Yes, those incompetent clerks have been at it again. Feeling a sudden spurt of patriotic fervor, I'm urging you to volunteer your spare time to help the Pentagon with its clerical tasks so this kind of error does not reoccur.

TrainING WarS

NATO admitted to having mistakenly bombed "a civilian vehicle" after Serbian television broadcast film of civilian corpses amidst burnt-out tractors. Sixty-four refugees reportedly died when a convoy of what appeared to be about 100 cars and tractors was bombed. NATO spokesman General Giuseppe Marani made a crucial advance in military logic when he announced that he could not account for the Serbian video. "I understand that tractors were filmed," he said. "Nevertheless, what I want to say is that when the pilot attacked the vehicles, they were military vehicles. If they turned out to be tractors, that is a different issue." Obviously the responsibility of another department. General Marani did not say if divine intervention was involved in this sudden conversion, but at a minimum it would appear we have a new criteria for what constitutes a military target.

Military-Industrial Logic 101

Traditionally, our citadels of higher learning have strived to avoid looking like mere storefronts for the Pentagon. But a report by the Natural Resources Defense Council criticized many major universities for their involvement in nuclear weapons research. The most visible target is a program at five universities to build a supercomputer to simulate the effects of nuclear explosions for the U.S. Energy Department. Fending off criticism of involving academia in the creation of weapons of mass destruction, Joan Rohlfing, a senior energy advisor to the Energy Department, made a fine distinction obviously missed by more fat-headed opponents. "The purpose of the department's simulation research financing," she said, "is to improve our ability to maintain the nation's nuclear stockpile, not to improve its performance." Should any improvements in performance occur by accident, the department would, of course, disregard them.

Our Embassies at Work

With the Cold War long dead and human rights out of fashion, do you sometimes wonder what our embassy employees actually do all day? Well, rest easy for they are hard at work promoting McDonald's, Boeing, and American business in general. *The Wall Street Journal* reported that American diplomats justify themselves to Congress and that junior officials enter the fast track for promotions on the strength of their record of business advocacy. This trend is credited to Lawrence Eagleburger, Secretary of State to George Bush, Sr., who issued an empowering Bill of Rights for U.S. business. In it he spelled out the policy that "executives had ... the right to have their views considered in foreign policy decisions." Does anyone need a translation here? Unfortunately, Eagleburger's policies on employee rights were inexplicably missing from my copy.

A Small Clarification

The Defense Department has been recycling old ammunition, making available over 100,000 rounds of armor-piercing .50 caliber shells for civilian use. The Pentagon has been selling the bullets to a company called Talon, possibly because the company, as you will see, speaks their lingo. Talon turns 98% of the bullets into scrap but is allowed to sell 2% to needy individuals and foreign governments such as those of Columbia and Brazil. At least that's what it looks like on the surface. In reality, things are a bit more complicated, as a company statement made clear: "Talon does not buy ammunition from the government but is paid by the government to demilitarize ammunition as established by contract." This leaves one with visions of a revival preacher saying, "Put your hands on the ammunition. By the power of the Holy Spirit, I say 'Demilitarize!'"

WHAT UPSETS THE PENTAGON

It's quiz time. Just read the following story and guess correctly what upset the Pentagon. The incident: Four-star Admiral Richard C. Macke had the crew of his Boeing 707 fly him from Hawaii to California, where he left them on standby while he took a three-day vacation with a female Marine lieutenant colonel. Was the Pentagon bothered by

(A) the $3,600 cost to taxpayers,
(B) lurid sex,
(C) unauthorized travel, or
(D none of the above?

The correct answer is (D). Their primary concern, and listen carefully, was that Admiral Macke had engaged in "an unduly familiar relationship" with a lower-ranking Navy officer. If she had only been of equal rank ... Hats off to the Navy for this advance in the language of intimacy. But wouldn't you love to be able to cross-examine one of their higher officers on the explicit differences, in naval terms, between an "unduly" and a "duly" familiar relationship? And if the name Richard Macke sounds familiar, it's because the same fellow gained a certain notoriety for chastising three sevicemen in an Okinawan rape case for not hiring a prostitute.

U.S. ARMY ATTACKED

The morale of 37,000 GIs in Korea was endangered by an ill-considered Defense Department decision. The Pentagon cut our troops' beer rations! Said U.S. Rep. Herbert Bateman (Va-R), "I don't like to see our troops over there not able to buy American beer that's important to their morale." How much beer per day do our troops need to keep up their morale? Try a case a day. Soldiers were previously allotted 30 cases each month of duty-free beer at $12 a case. Now they can only buy eight per month, or a measly eight bottles of Bud a day! The Beer Institute immediately recognized the injustice and pushed the U.S. House to demand the Army justify the new policy and explain how it planned to make up for lost beer revenue. Thomas Doherty, spokesperson for Anheuser-Busch, warned the Pentagon's beer policy "subverts the exchange business to the whims or moral dictates of a local military authority." Besides the sanctity of the market issue, it's kind of scary to think our soldiers might be out defending us with anything less than a full case of beer in their guts.

SENSITIVITY TRAINING — ARMY STYLE

No doubt many of you worry whether the generals of our U.S. Army are able to take advantage of the many advances being made today by our high-powered motivational industry. I'm glad to report that 81 of our finest generals were able to participate in a week-long Brigadier General Training Course, where they were taught how to get in touch with their "inner jerk" by Lt. Col. Howard Olsen. The Colonel may have verged on divulging classified information when he told the assembled generals that "each and every one of you has something that makes you a jerk." Later, another unnamed general spoke out about the treaty banning landmines. He warned, "That's the first step on the road to disarmament. The next step is to go after your M-16s." Obviously, this general's efforts to get in touch with his inner jerk were a complete success.

Helpful Hints

Sometimes conformity with the government is for the best. Several months after September 11th, House Republican leader Scott McInnis sent a letter to environmental organizations demanding they "publicly disavow the actions of ecoterrorist organizations" like the Earth Liberation Front and the Animal Liberation Front. Many groups, I'm sure, reacted with knee-jerk rejections of such McCarthyism. But Ray Vaughn, director of an environmental law firm named Wildlaw, wrote back to "join" the cause. Said he: "We have long fought against those secretive multinational organizations that have sponsored 'environmental terrorism' in America. Throughout our great land, these groups are poisoning our air, our water, and our food supply." Noting how un-American it was to terrorize the environment, Wildlaw applauded Rep. McInnis for his "heroic efforts." I'm sure their support was more than welcome. Thanks to the Internet, Wildlaw's "patriotic" example was shared with countless citizens — who hopefully will find their own ways of combating the real terrorists.

A Groucho Marxist Response

"This is a fine kettle of fish you've gotten us into."

— Stan Laurel and Oliver Hardy

Comparisons of America to the Roman Empire are obvious but often too easily come by. But one such analogy, by Alastair MacIntyre, a British philosopher, rather neatly sums up the lessons of our Newspeak-littered public life. In his book *After Virtue*, MacIntyre tells us that a "crucial turning point in that earlier history occurred when men and women of good will turned aside from the task of shoring up the Roman imperium ..." They withdrew from the civic life of their day, he says, and without really knowing what they were about, constructed new and smaller forms of community able to withstand the coming tides of barbarism. Much like today, except for one important difference. "This time," writes MacIntyre, "the barbarians are not waiting beyond the frontiers; they have already been governing us for some time. And it is our lack of consciousness of this that constitutes part of our predicament."

Today's dangerous barbarians are not the hate-filled racists hiding out in the hills of Idaho or in sheriff's offices in Alabama or in caves in Afghanistan. Nor are they the expletive-laden rappers of our inner cities. We should be so lucky. No, the real barbarians are self-important executives armed with highly educated, razor-sharp, latte-sodden minds capable of looking at any peaceful meadow and dissecting it into parking lots, condominiums, drive-in churches, and ad campaigns for a new improved "Peaceful Meadows." Our barbarians come armed not with anger, but with shallowness, shortsightedness, and indifference.

The public landscape is littered with Newspeak partly because of the "vacation" from civic involvement too many of us have been taking. Since 1960, as Robert Putman has shown in his important book *Bowling Alone*, virtually every measurement of participation in community life from PTA attendance to Kiwanis Club membership to bowling league participation shows us dropping off the charts. Putnam discovered that "more than a third of America's civic infrastructure simply evaporated between the mid-1970s and the mid-1990s." This is like a 98-pound weakling going on a 20-calorie diet. As Americans hunker down into their cocoons with their VCRs, multinational corporations, the media and bureaucracies have been left free to extend their logics unhindered by organized communities. The erosion of grass-roots democracy and community involvement is the flipside to the growth of Newspeak.

If this collection of gnarled Orwellian logic and language butchering I've presented didn't leave you clawing up the walls, you're probably wondering what can be done. The degree to which corporations and bureaucracies are colonizing every inch of our daily life can feel overwhelming. The willingness of people and institutions to build higher and higher walls around themselves and to live in greater denial, whether from privilege or pain, can feel dispiriting. Where does that leave us? What brilliant ideas does this underpaid curmudgeon of an author have for returning a bit of sanity to public discourse? Is he going to tell me to write a letter to my congressperson or newspaper editor or something equally exciting? Snore.

Yes, I am. But I'm here to say try making it funny. Just try. There are times for anger, there are times for outrage, but there are also times for ridicule, satire, parody, and play. Frankly, the world has had enough of whiney tones from progressives with a cause. The quota has been filled. The time has come for Groucho Marxism, for using more humor to undermine, to deconstruct the "wallage" from which Newspeak grows and to help inject some life into our communities. The twin peaks of capitalism and bureaucracy are guaranteed to be producing mounting piles of absurdities for all of our lifetimes. There will be no shortage of material. That said, I'd like to look at the deeper foundations of the overproduction of the Absurd. Why are we destined for thicker and thicker layers of Newspeak?

There is a real chink in the armor of our corporate, consumer-driven new world order, an Achilles heel from which the absurdities flow. It won't sound like much and it certainly didn't to me the first time I heard the sociologist Robert Bellah make the point. I remember Bellah telling an audience in Seattle that the whole "looking out for number one" mentality, the whole idea that we are unique individuals separate from or standing above the world about us (the premise undergirding Newspeak) was based on what the sciences are realizing is an epistemological mistake, a fundamental error in the unconscious metaphors that frame the way we see the world.

As a commercial fisherman recently returned from Alaska, I responded with a "Thank God for liberals. What a nice polite way of describing the worldview of self-absorbed yuppies. I wish I could talk like that." On the docks, we had other, slightly more colorful phrases to describe our narcissistic upwardly mobile brothers and sisters. I imagined myself telling my halibut fishing crew, "Hey gang, I'm sorry. I made an epistemological mistake. There'll be no fishing today." But years later when, to my surprise, I had a small taste of the boundaries between myself and the natural world melting away in the practice of meditation, Bellah's contention took on a lot more force.

Ever since biologists first unpacked the concept of "ecology," we've been forced inescapably to the view that we too are an integral part of nature, just like every traditional Native American culture has taught for millennia. In the industrial paradigm, humans stood apart from nature and each other as solitary atoms, each with their separate values, rights, and property. From imperial heights we measured and analyzed the world and the races beneath us. But ecology has shattered such hierarchical snobbishness, revealing the totally separate self as an expensive delusion. The walls we've built with suburban homes, new BMWs, administrative memos, career promotions, etc., are all defending a self that's a remnant of the 19th century machine age, a disconnected tourist self complete with two spoiled kids in the back of a station wagon whining about the absence of TV.

If it is true that the separate ego is an illusion, a denial of its own social formation, then we are on a slippery slide toward feeling our interconnectedness first with others, then with broader circles of life. Soon we are prone to hugging trees and animals and rocks and even stone-age Republicans, calling them our long-lost brothers and sisters. If we are all particular manifestations of the same humanity or nature or life force, then we've been living walled off from the obvious. We open ourselves to a world where "an injury to one is," in fact, "an injury to all." We've been raising defensive shields against our own natural selves and it's time to go off red alert and to open the store to others and the world about us.

Once you've penetrated those walls and rejoined the world, you are in the driver's seat. That's because you don't have to lug around a fake ID, an empty, isolated self that needs to be fed continuously with new toys and tokens of prestige. You don't have to block out your connectedness to the species our lifestyles are destroying or to millions of Third World people whose lives are squandered producing the toys we demand on sale at Costco. You're free of that excess baggage, free of untold layers of denial, free to unplug your TV, free to penetrate the institutional and personal walls of those around you, free to run out in the streets, like a chastened Mr. Scrooge, and buy a turkey for Tiny Tim.

Turning to the other side, those in power who've bought this worthless clunker of a paradigm have a problem. As they become more and more abstract, they get cut off from their own selves, their emotions, their bodies, their families and friends. As they get more out of touch, their capacity to generate Newspeak goes up exponentially. Pure capitalist rationality, for example, has no means for opposing child labor. Why shouldn't we exploit those willing little productive units? Except for my child, of course. Capitalism "works" only because it doesn't follow its own logic out to the bitter end. It's held on a leash. But when the little pit bull is let loose, we just have to sit back and harvest the absurdities it will create on its own.

The key term in all of this is *penetrate*. Once we're able to see the evolving language of advertising executives or Pentagon planners as the discourse of the epistemologically challenged, our job changes. The mind that can view a dead child as "collateral damage" needs more than just additional data presented. As we've learned from Freud, Wittgenstein, Piaget, Foucault, and a host of other thinkers, knowledge is not about the piling up of isolated facts. Knowledge is about constructing paradigms, gestalts, language games, and systems. Words and facts take on their meanings within largely unconscious cultural frameworks. In a culture that takes witchcraft for granted, efforts by you to disprove it can only be taken as evidence of your bewitchment. Likewise in a narcissistic culture, opposition can only be comprehended as self-seeking. It's this circularity or flat one-dimensionality of the Newspeakian worldview — built upon distancing, disconnecting, and denying — that we need to pierce with our humor-laced darts.

Even granting that we have a materialistic culture that has arrogantly driven up an epistemological dead end, what are we to do beyond collecting samples of Newspeak like butterflies and chuckling? How do we get beyond running up to mentally gridlocked administrators and shouting, "You flunked Epistemology 101, nyah-nyah-na-na-nyah." (Although do it if it works!) And how do we keep our humor from becoming mean-spirited? Here is where I'd suggest you might want to go out and get yourself a mentor in this field. That's what I did. Admittedly, he's not much of a guru figure, kind of a KMart version, but he's the best I could come up with on short notice. So relax and let me tell you this story about a very special friend of mine and the reason I ended up becoming a follower of his.

My moral guide was a big, chubby smiling eleven-year-old boy, whom I will call Roberto. He was a student in a learning-disabled class in a middle school in Seattle where I worked. This moon-faced youth had come to this country from Mexico three years earlier and spoke his English as if walking on eggs. His actions displayed the same care and were usually preceded by timidly framed requests for permission, using such foreign phrases as "please," "thank you," and "may I." Academically, he struggled to read third-grade texts and needed his fingers to solve problems like 8 plus 5. He'd say "I'm sorry" when he missed a math problem, despite our best efforts to convince him that mistakes in addition were not considered crimes in our country. His greatest joy was playing games where he'd sneak up on me, tap me on the shoulder, and hide behind my back as I turned to find him. Day after day after day we played it.

One day Roberto came up to me and said, "You know what, Mr. G? You are my very best friend." But soon I overheard him expressing the same words to the teacher I worked with, Ms. Cathy O'Leary. Then I heard him address the same words to at least two other students. It was a short tenure as his very best friend, I thought. Now came one of my lowest points as an educator (the competition is surprisingly tough here). Assuming that taxpayers expected me to make at least a pretense of teaching, I decided I'd actually try to instruct him in the proper use of the phrase "very best friend." So bringing out my best Mr. Rogers voice I carefully explained how we use the phrase "very best friend" with a certain economy in our culture. Roberto nodded that he understood and then went about his business.

The very next day, while I was busy resting on my laurels, I watched as Roberto walked up to two of our P.E. teachers who were standing together. First Roberto put his arm around the closest teacher and said, "You know what? You are my very best friend." Then he walked a few paces to the other teacher, again placed his arm around the shoulder and said, "You know what? You are my very best friend." As I watched the two men blush beet red (a fact I'm sure they would deny), it dawned on me that Roberto wasn't just misusing the language, he was saying precisely what he meant. And he was connecting with people. Deeply, openly, honestly, infectiously, touching them in a way I can only hope he won't lose as his sophistication in the ways of our culture increases. I watched over the months as Roberto initiated more teachers and students into the growing circle of "very best friends." I thought, as I watched, "He's got it. What more do you need? To hell with fancy religions or ethical philosophies, I'll just follow this kid and save a bundle."

The moral thought of Western civilization centers around the concept of justice (or fairness). It assumes a world of individual property holders who have certain rights. The moral individual is the person who can see the perspectives of others and fairly and dispassionately weigh competing claims to the societal pie. Psychologists like Lawrence Kohlberg have found that moral reasoning can be measured and divided into clear stages. Confronted with a moral dilemma like whether or not it's proper to steal to save a life, people make choices in framing the problem that show a clear progression from concrete fears of punishment to concern over how friends will view them to concerns about societal law and order to abstract reasoning about justice.

Critics like psychologist Carol Gilligan have pointed to the male bias in this picture and have argued that we also need to focus on the concepts of care and responsibility to others. Roberto, I believe, points even further. This youth possesses a gift that does not show up on tests of moral reasoning (surprise, surprise). It's a gift shared by most respected spiritual leaders, namely the ability to cut through society's cow excrement, to slice through the roles and masks we wear and, with complete simplicity, to point right to the heart. It's seen, for example, in St. Francis of Assisi's disarmingly simple practice of addressing objects in the natural world as "Brother Wind," Sister Moon," or "Brother Donkey." It's a quality we either grant sainthood for or a nice padded cell.

Allow me one more story, this time from the early Civil Rights movement as recounted by David Halberstam in his wonderful history of the period called *The Children*. In Nashville, at the time of the first lunch counter sit-ins in 1960, a group of rednecks attacked and beat up two of the young college protesters marching to the local Woolworth's. The mentor of these students, the Rev. James Lawson, walked over to the attackers and was promptly spat upon for his efforts. Lawson calmly asked for a handkerchief and, noting the fine motorcycle jacket worn by the man, started asking questions about the man's cycle. Soon the two were off discussing horsepower and ways to customize bikes. And while the injured protesters quietly rejoined the march, Lawson was still discussing Harleys with the leader of the whites.

Simply, almost effortlessly, Rev. Lawson had cut through their differences. He didn't exactly say, "You are my very best friend." He just said that they were both human and that they both liked motorcycles. That's all.

It's the same "words" that so many fire fighters said with their lives as they ran into the World Trade Center. Who knew the risk better? Who among them turned back? In times of disaster, when we fail to "think," we betray a reality of connectedness to one another that soon dissipates as "normality" returns and we "freeze" our experience as patriotism or religion. After the jet hit the Pentagon, even Secretary of Defense David Rumsfeld was out helping victims before his "responsibilities" as a top official dawned on him. Or when we are in love, we also catch a partial glimpse of connectedness as our ego boundaries melt

"You are my very best friend" may not be very funny, but it cuts right through all of our society's bullshit. (It even started to cut through mine.) If Newspeak is about adding layer upon layer of distancing and denial of our common roots, then the answer would have to be directly connecting with people, and that is what our humor must do. That simple practice is the first step in rebuilding community. The next steps, if you are feeling really audacious, are asking the root questions "Can you come out and play?" or "Can you come out and join the world, as an equal?"

This is said in place of our culture's root sentences "What can you do for me?" and "How much does that cost?" and "Take a number and form a line to the left." And when a whole group of people turn to each other and say "You are my very best friend," then you have a community or even a movement (just like folksinger Arlo Guthrie's Alice's Restaurant movement, except you needn't sing in four-part harmony). In a society that has turned every relation into a commodity, there it is: Thoughtcrime. Subversion, right in your own home, school, or workplace.

Offering friendship, simply being totally present for someone with no thought of gain — these "survivals" from our past have now become radical acts challenging the premises of a consumer- and career-driven society. Most of us picture a radical as an angry strident militant marching in the streets with an upraised clenched fist. There are times when that may be necessary. But let's not pretend it's radical. It remains action grounded in a false sense of separation. It's usually closer to the posturing done in professional wrestling. The tougher task is to connect with the people you are challenging. That is where humor, I'm told, can play an important role in dissolving blockages, in deconstructing or, as I prefer to say, de-wallaging. That's how we "build the form of the new society within the shell of the old," as the Wobblies used to say.

Roberto's "You are my very best friend" is but one example of what Buddhist practitioners would refer to as "skillful means" (*upaya*) to unlock minds artificially separated from the world. Among the most famous techniques are the koans of the Zen tradition. For example, in one case, the Zen Master Joshu was asked about the ultimate meaning of reality. Pointing to a nearby tree, he responded, "The oak tree in the garden." Slice. The Zen Master Gutei answered the same question by silently holding up one finger. No intellectual constructs, no separation, no self, no object, just IT. You're IT. Total simplicity and directness, leaving students with the task of penetrating and manifesting Joshu's "oak tree" or Gutei's "one finger," even when the finger has been cut off.

As obscure as koans may appear on the surface, their central intent of penetrating blockages to human development is implicit in all the better traditions of political mobilization from Gandhi to America's own grandfather of community organizing, Saul Alinski. In *Rules for Radicals*, Alinsky's official guidebook to rabblerousing, the central insight is that we need to avoid engaging in professional wrestling with corporations and the state and to resort to political jujitsu or aikido instead. This means yielding "in such planned and skilled ways that the superior strength of the Haves becomes their undoing," as it did in the South when fire hoses and police dogs were turned loose on children in Montgomery by the infamous Bull Conner. In a nutshell, the rules boil down to the dictum "Go outside the experience of the enemy, stay inside the experience of your people." For example, in Seattle a large group of poor and homeless people who had experienced the city's lack of public accommodations suddenly discovered they needed to use bathroom facilities all at the same time. So they went to a nearby Nordtstrom's and a Bon Marché and lined up to use their facilities, unfortunately blocking the aisles for many shoppers. We can only pray they did not upset the sensibilities of more refined customers. Two years later the city council actually moved on the issue, something of a record.

The chief problem is that once a tactic is used repeatedly, "it ceases to be outside the experience of the enemy." This is the same problem Captain Picard and the Star Trek crew faced when battling the Borg. Obviously, what is commonly known as the Left has been breaking these rules for the past thirty years. This will not look good on their résumés. Tired tactics are a damn good sign that activists have retreated behind their own walls and have become weighed down with defensive armor just like the bureaucrats they confront.

There is no requirement that politics be dull and boring. Given our addiction to televised entertainment, rule number one is that public meetings need to provide as much sustenance as *Hollywood Squares*. Creativity, play, and humor are the banana peels that trip up the victims of mental gridlock running our society. They also make political involvement satisfying and, at times, even uplifting. For example, faced with the problem of advertisers invading public education through Channel One and now through Internet banners on school computers, you can become enraged, write a protest letter, form an organization to oppose commercialization in schools, picket a school board meeting, etc. Or you could "accept" the commercial logic and "demand" more freedom for advertisers, classes on becoming better consumers, inclusion of advertising jingles in standardized tests, ad breaks between classes, etc. Then announce with appropriately mindless smiles that your group is sponsored by Pepsi-Cola and bring out free drinks for everyone. The first tactic will probably work fine if you gather enough people. Politics is mainly physics after all. Don't read me wrong, I'm not disdaining more conventional forms of activism. Our biggest problem these days is isolation and disconnection, and any tactic that brings people together to oppose of out time, no matter how unimaginative it may feel, needs our support and involvement. But the second tactic strikes at the heart. It's jujitsu or aikido, taking the logic of the opponent and extending it just a few tiny steps until its absurdities become transparent to all.

Many of you should remember Michael Moore's unsuccessful efforts to sit down and have a chat over coffee with the head of General Motors about why he shut down the auto factory in Flint, Michigan, as documented in his film *Roger and Me*. Moore has patented a style of just being a neighborly small-town Gomer Pyle in the midst of complex social hierarchies. Upon hearing, for example, that Bill and Melinda Gates had moved into their mansion, Moore invited people to join a traditional welcoming wagon to help the newlyweds. The hundreds of friendly neighbors bearing simple gifts were rather rudely shooed away by security guards. Very educational.

The model of aikido, of using stronger opponents' strengths against them, has led to experiments in "turning" advertising and the media, known as the culture jamming movement. Culture jammers use advertising's own tools to help display how we are manipulated or to convey an alternative to our constant bombardment with corporate messages. Groups like the Billboard Liberation Front have made "improveming" on outdoor advertising a national pastime. So far the record holder in this division appears to be a Chicago group called Operation Clean that "refaced" over 1000 cigarette and alcohol billboards in one year alone. Or look at John DeGraf's hilarious use of fifties advertising to debunk consumerism in the PBS documentary *Affluenza*. Or Negativland's CD *Dyspepsia*, consisting of snippets of Pepsi commercial jingles, repeated ad nauseum. Or the fine parody ads of the Adbusters group out of Canada, promoters of the TV network-censored Buy Nothing Day. All are fine models of Thoughtcrime, of the festive reclaiming of public space, of Alinski's Rule No. 4: "Ridicule is man's most potent weapon. It is almost impossible to counterattack ridicule. Also it infuriates the opposition, who then react to your advantage."

One advantage of the fact that Newspeak has spread deeper into the sinews of our society is that it makes subversion ever so much easier. Once having a simple conversation with a sales clerk was an everyday affair. Now when you get in line at a Burger King or a McDonald's, where the clerk's time spent per customer is measured, an overlong discussion of the weather with a "rebellious" clerk can be counted as subversion. Better yet, just don't buy anything. Very subversive. Refusing to smile at the surveillance cameras when there are signs telling you to do so. Très dangereux. Actually turning off your TV set, spending time camping when you could be working overtime, seducing fast-track upwardly mobile students with poetry and late-night discussions of philosophy. Or following directions to the letter at work, or creating new totally pointless forms to be filled out in triplicate. The possibilities are endless.

This all may sound like fun but there is a downside. Becoming a productive subversive means freeing yourself from years of conditioning. It means developing a practice, putting in the "reps," to counter a lifetime of training to manipulate others and to amass toys. This is the hurdle most hippies and activists from my generation of the sixties failed to clear. Whether it be Roberto's greeting, meditation or prayer, choral singing or chanting, communing with mountains and Douglas firs, volunteering at foodbanks, folk or tribal dancing — we are all in need of the cooperative practices developed in traditional cultures to reconnect us to nature and our brothers and sisters. Ecopsychologist Chellis Glendinning says it all in her book title *My Name is Chellis and I'm in Recovery From Western Civilization*. She suggests a twelve-step AA-style program to help us recover from consumer addictions. How long? Figure the number of hours you've spent passively in front of a TV set. Then multiply by ...

Fortunately, becoming a speaker of Newspeak is not an easy job either. If it is true that we are all interconnected with one another and nature, then maintaining a narcissistic identity cut off from the world requires suppressing major parts of our larger self and of what teachers, friends, and family have "invested" in us. In the right hands, creativity, play, and humor can address the suppressed sides, including the inner-children living inside even the most soul-less public relations executive. We have allies behind corporate and administrative facades — human beings waiting to peck their way out of their shells. "Something there is that does not love a wall ..." said the poet Robert Frost. This was Gandhi's insight. This was Martin Luther King, Jr.'s strength. This is Groucho Marxism. Go for it.

Endnotes

Excuse me, but this is primarily a satirical book and not a PhD thesis, so count yourself lucky with the citations you find here. Hopefully, a few of the quotations you read will leave you wondering, "Who could have dreamt up this cow excrement?" So I've provided original sources for at least the Newspeak-worthy remarks. Here are the abbreviations I used:

AA — *Advertising Age*
AD — *American Demographics*
AP — Associated Press
BG — *The Boston Globe*
BW — *Business Week*
CR — *The Congressional Record*
FMG — *Fernwood Moose-Gazette*
LAT — *The Los Angeles Times*
N — *The Nation*
NYT — *The New York Times*
R — Reuters
SFC — *The San Francisco Chronicle*
SPI — *The Seattle Post-Intelligencer*
ST — *The Seattle Times*
WP — *The Washington Post*
WSJ — *The Wall Street Journal*

1: THE DEPTHS OF SHALLOWNESS

Tourist Meccas (NYT, 5/26/96; WSJ, 10/17/97)

Quality Time with Nature (WSJ, 7/8/97)

Airhead Protection Dept. (BG, 10/15/98; NYT, 12/26/94)

Barbie's Bad Day (ST, 6/7/97)

The Tightening Circle (WSJ, 1/20/98)

Designer Marxism (NYT, 4/30/97; AP, 3/22/98)

New Frontiers in Intimacy   (SPI, 7/12/96; Reuters, 12/27/95)

Bible Improvements (NYT, 10/28/96)

Defending the Fatherland (WP, 2/6/99; AP, 8/14/97)

Buy American (NYT, 4/16/98)

Dumbing Down Dept. (AP, 10/8/99)

A Dog's Best Friend (NYT, 3/22/98)

Revenge of the Nerds (WSJ, 5/19/99)

Kiss of Death (WP, 3/17/99)

2: THE EDUCATION MALL

Two-Way Discourse (*Adbusters*, 1/01)

A Place in the Sun (Brunico press release, 5/2/01)

Baby Wars (WSJ, 1/9/01)

Preschool Outreach (WSJ, 10/28/96)

Defenders of Childhood (LAT, 9/9/01)

New-Age Role Models (NYT, 1/28/01)

Power to the Little People (NYT, 4/5/99)

Empowering Our Schools (WSJ, 9/15/97)

Subversion Is Everywhere (NYT, 3/10/98, 3/16/98)

New Math (AP, 3/24/99)

Upstairs, Downstairs (WSJ, 12/17/98)

Let Them Study Cake Dept. (NYT, 4/20/97)

Son of Reefer Madness (NYT, 5/8/97)

Improving the Past (AP, 6/21/98, 6/24/99)

Bureaucracy Appreciation 101 (NYT, 10/3/96; ST, 10/2/96)

"A Rose by any Other Name ..." (WSJ, 1/23/01)

3. CLASS FRONTIERS

Out of the Closet (NYT, 12/12/96)

Pleasantville (WSJ, 10/7/98)

Happy Endings (WSJ, 3/4/99)

New Entitlements (WSJ, 5/1/98; BG, 12/26/99)

"Ain't Going Door-to-Door No More ..." (ST, 2/17/00)

Social Climbing 101 (WSJ, 12/11/98, 10/15/00)

Friendly Skies (BW, 2/23/98)

Shortages Hit Even the Affluent (WSJ, 9/26/97)

Wall Street Angst (WSJ, 12/1/96)

Going Native (WSJ, 5/26/99)

Small Ain't Beautiful No More (US News & World Report, 3/2/98)

Silver Spoon Dept. (NYT *Magazine*, 12/18/00)

4: AD NATION

Ad Agency Phobias (WSJ, 5/30/97)

Inner City Beautification (WS, Jl/10/01; WSJ, 1/27/95)

How to Advertise Your Assault Guns (ST, 9/7/01; Violence Policy Center report, www.vpc.org/studies/smalint.htm)

Charlie Gets Hip (NYT, 9/16/96)

Gen X Ads Go Negative (BW, 8/11/97)

Drawing the Line (AP, 3/7/97)

Beyond Upscale (WSJ, 7/30/97)

Phillip Morris Does "The Woman Thing" (WSJ, 1/15/97)

Facing the Challenge (NYT, 10/20/97)

Sponsored Conversations (LT, 3/13/97; WSJ, 4/21/99)

Final Sanctuary (WSJ, 9/29/97)

New, Improved Moon (R, 10/27/97)

Take back the Night (WSJ, 2/23/99)

Final Barriers Dept. (AD, 5/98)

"What's that in the sky ...?" (WSJ, 11/10/98)

Deep Thoughts (WSJ, 12/24/98)

Empowerment Update (WSJ, 3/20/97)

Friendly Firearms (WSJ, 4/5/99)

5: MEDIASPEAK

The New Journalism (FAIR press release, 9/01; www.mediare-lations.com)

Emperor's Clothing Dept. (AA, 11/11/96)

Objective Cheerleading (*The Sydney Morning Herald*, 11/18/01, WSJ, 9/21/01)

Raising the Bar (ST, 11/30/99)

Craft Pride Returns (WSJ, 8/6/97)

Muckraking Press (WSJ, 11/18/97; NYT, 5/18/98)

Literary Pioneer (NYT, 9/13/01)

Writers Improve Their IQs (NYT, 10/27/97)

Crumbling Walls (WSJ, 4/19/99)

Cutting-Edge Comics (AA, 10/6/97)

"Sometimes a Great Notion" (WSJ, 2/9/99; NYT, 2/8/99; WSJ, 2/7/01)

History Rewriting 101 (SPI, 11/14/97; WSJ, 6/25/99)

TV Fills the Void (WP, 5/5/97)

New, Improved PBS (WSJ, 7/3/96; AA, 12/18/97)

Nature Abhors a Vacuum   (NYT, 4/6/99; WSJ, 7/30/98, NYT, 5/23/01)

Sponsor-Friendly TV Programs   (WSJ, 8/24/01, WSJ, 7/12/00; WSJ, 3/25/97)

Defending the Constitution (WSJ, 3/17/97)

Movie Upgrades (WP, 5/13/99)

Monopoly Benefits Us All (WSJ, 9/18/97)

6: POSTMODERN CENSORSHIP

Advanced Numbing (NYT, 9/19/01)

Spreading the Virus (WP, 11/19/01)

Activist Playgrounds (AP, 8/1/01; WP, 10/27/96)

Buy Nothing Day (WSJ, 11/19/97)

Too Many Big Words (R, 12/23/00)

"Just Say No" Dept. (*Solidarity*, 3/99)

"First they came for the Communists, and I didn't speak up..." (AP, 4/18/97)

Student Censorship Made Simple (AP, 9/7/97)

7: DEPARTMENT OF DOWNSIZING

New Work Environments (WSJ, 5/12/98; WSJ, 9/16/97)

Best Downsizings of an Individual (NYT, 12/18/96; ST, 4/4/96)

Best Firings by a Public Agency (*The Gaston Gazette*, 9/14/99; ST, 10/18/96)

New Ways to Raise Productivity (Nando.net, 9/25/97)

8: CORPORATESPEAK

CEO Pioneer Awards (NYT, 2/22/96; WSJ, 3/27/97; WSJ, 4/7/97)

Global Attitude Adjustment Time (WSJ, 5/26/98)

New-Age CEOs (WSJ, 4/22/98)

Who Do You Trust? (BW, 2/8/00)

Corporate Crime Report (*Fortune*, 4/14/97; BW, 4/14/97)

Welfare Mothers Respond (NYT, 2/2/97; WSJ, 1/17/97)

Einstein to the Rescue (NYT, 10/24/96)

"I Have a Dream" Dept (AP, 11/9/97)

Loan Sharks Go Respectable (*Village Voice*, 7/15/97)

Beyond Breastfeeding (WSJ, 6/18/99)

McChildcare (NYT, 5/4/97)

Bank Refuses to "Close" (LAT, 4/10/97)

Donut Fever (WSJ, 8/30/99)

Sharks Eating Sharks Dept. (*Portland Oregonian*, 2/23/99)

Microspeak Version 4.1 (*Manual of Style for Technical Publications*, 2nd ed., 1998, p. 185)

Happy Thoughts (TechWeb, 3/20/98; WSJ, 1/27/99)

9: MCHEALTH AND SCIENCE-MART

Philip Morris Sees the Light (Arthur D. Little, *Public Finance Balance of Smoking in the Czech Republic*, 11/28/01)

Scientific Groundswell (*Opelika-Auburn News*, 3/12/97; NYT, 10/17/97)

Cereal Killers (WSJ, 1/2/98)

Used Science for Sale (WP, 6/19/98)

"Twas brillig and the slithy toves ..." (NYT, 2/20/97)

Big Mac Health Care (N, 11/18/96; WSJ, 5/28/97; WSJ, 2/6/00)

Affordable Health Care (ST, 8/19/96)

General Hospital Goes Deluxe (WSJ, 9/16/96)

New-Age Hospital Care (NYT, 4/14/96)

Doctors Find Their True Calling (WSJ, 6/18/97)

"And a Free Toaster with Each Appendectomy" (BW, 12/8/97)

Psycho: The Ad (WSJ, 2/10/98; NYT, 2/17/98; AD, 10/98)

Auditors to the Rescue (LAT, 3/15/97)

White Gummy Liquid Dept. (WSJ, 1/6/00)

10: LEGAL DISORDERS

Defending the Homeland (LAT, 6/29/01)

The Con Goes On (WSJ, 5/25/99)

McPrison Raises Its Standards (N, 1/5/98)

Return of the Keystone Cops (SPI, 11/6/96)

New Standards for Punishment (AP, 3/25/97; NYT, 3/27/97)

Upholding Community Standards (AP, 4/9/97; WP, 4/10/97)

No Free Lunch Dept. (R, 8/29/97)

Wilderness Justice Returns (NYT, 8/31/97)

Having Your Cake and Eating It Too (WSJ, 10/8/98; AP, 12/12/98; NYT, 12/22/98)

Letter of the Law Dept. (AP, 11/7/98)

Bureaucracy in Action (WSJ, 3/24/99)

The Naked City (NYT, 5/13/99)

Cool Hand Luke Update (AP, 6/16/99)

Not All God's Children (ACLU press release, 10/1/99)

Global Jail (www.spacer.com, 4/8/98)

Support Your Local Federal Judge (SPI, 10/8/96)

Wrong Turns (www.itsonlycigars.com)

Why I Want to Be a Lawyer (WSJ, 10/7/96)

11: BIG BROTHERDOM

Making a Better World (WSJ, 9/21/01; CR, HR 3162; www.timesrecord.com, 12/17/01)

The Blind Leading the Blind (www.goacta.org)

Attitude Adjustment Time (TechWire, 9/25/97)

New Wine in Old Wine Bags Dept. (R, 2/14/01)

Son of Star Wars (NYT, 3/2/01)

Rent a Spy Satellite (NYT, 2/10/97)

Do-It-Yourself Spy Kits (R, 11/21/97)

Big Brother Visits the Washroom (WSJ, 5/20/97; AP, 5/20/97)

Little Brothers on the Net (Knight-Ridder, 3/11/97)

Smile and Shut Up Dept. (NYT, 3/2/99; R, 7/31/00)

Death of a Salesman   (Knight-Ridder, 5/28/97; WSJ, 4/24/97; AA, 7/14/97; AD, 11/98)

Turn in Your Parents Dept. (WSJ, 6/9/97)

Child Protection Report Card (SFC, 3/27/97; AP, 3/26/97)

Going Beyond Mere Privacy (NYT, 6/12/97)

Employee Recognition (AP, 5/22/97; WP, 5/24/97)

Privatizing Big Brother (WSJ, 9/2/97)

New, Improved Freedom of Speech (NYT, 9/30/99)

Return of Air Safety (NYT, 12/31/97)

"Smile, You're on Candid Camera" (NYT, 2/22/98)

Feeling Naked (WP, 3/3/98)

Special Agents Dept. (NYT, 4/29/99)

Police State Lite (AP, 6/17/99)

12: GREENWASH

Going Green Made Simple (www.awg.org/home/clear/players/4197.html)

Nuclear Power Goes Clean (New Republic, 11/30/98; New Yorker, 4/23/01)

Tree Hugging Dept. (www.greeningearthsociety.org)

Almost-Environmental Activism (ST, 2/19/96)

Grass-roots Fertilizers (www.apcoassoc.com)

Vanishing Acts (Wired News, 3/23/01; www.wired.com/news/politics/0,1283,42536,00.html)

Clearing the Waters (NYT, 12/29/98)

Defending Our Inner Cities (NYT, 5/10/98)

"Organic" Gets a Face Lift (WP, 1/1/98)

Off to the Glue Factory (AP, 3/22/97)

New Spin on Trees (CR, HR 2458)

Fairness for Logging Companies (AP, 5/15/97)

Ending Pollution (ST, 3/9/98)

Helpful Hints (www.corporatewatch.org)

13: ASTROTURF POLITICS

"Ask not what your country can do for you ..." (WP, 11/11/01)

Fashion Statements (WP, 3/9/01)

Exporting Democracy (*Time*, 7/15/96)

Support for Political Participation (NYT, 6/24/96; CR, 3/12/97)

It Never Happened Here (WP, 3/7/97)

Dinner Prices in Washington, D.C. (NYT, 12/27/96; ST, 1/29/97)

Mom and Apple Pie Dept. (NYT, 2/20/97; LAT, 2/22/97)

Investing In America (ST, 1/24/97)

Endowments for Democracy (NYT, 3/31/97)

Stealth Campaign (*Newsweek*, 11/18/96)

Fellowship in High Places (NYT, 5/17/97)

New Civil Rights (WSJ, 1/24/97)

Welfare Slashing Made Simple (WP, 3/14/97)

Where's Forrest Gump? (WSJ, 6/20/96)

Selling the War on Drugs (WP, 4/30/98)

Special Interest Watchers (WP, 9/30/96; WSJ, 10/1/96)

"But Everybody's Doing It" (SFC, 9/16/97; WSJ, 12/21/98)

Helpful Hints (WTO press release, 10/30/01)

14: BUREAU-ARTHRITIS

Introduction (R, 12/30/98)

Advanced Flag Waving (CR, 10/24/01)

"Who's on First ..." (NYT, 10/28/01)

Chip Off the Old Block Dept. (WSJ, 10/5/00)

New, Improved Government (WP, 3/8/99; www.brook.edu)

Political Upgrade (NPR, *All Things Considered*, 4/17/97; WSJ, 1/11/01)

"Of Human Bondage" (NYT, 10/1/97)

"If you can't be with the one you love ..." (WP, 10/2/99)

Foreign Service Goes Scientific (Knight-Ridder, 6/8/97)

The Full Monty Rules (NYT, 4/10/98)

The IRS Stands and Delivers (LAT, 2/14/97)

Coming-out Party (WSJ, 1/11/01)

Setting the Bar Higher (NYT, 8/29/97)

15: PERMA-WAR

War Marketing (http://www.rendon.com)

Perception Management (Rambo Division) (www.milinfos-erv.net/BMO.htm)

Advanced Finger Pointing (DoD press releases, 10/07/0, 10/24/01)

Educational Achievements (NYT, 4/3/95; WP, 9/21/96; BS, 1/27/97)

Price Quotes on Children (*60 Minutes*, 5/12/96)

Criminal Conspiracies Dept. (www.nonviolence.org/vitw, 12/3/98)

Selling Arms to our Friends (NYT, 8/2/97; NYT, 1/20/97)

The Real Gulf War Syndrome (NYT, 9/6/96; ST, 9/12/96)

Training Wars (R, 4/15/99)

Military-Industrial Logic 101 (NYT, 1/25/98)

Our Embassies at Work (WSJ, 1/21/97)

A Small Clarification (AP, 6/16/99)

What Upsets the Pentagon (WP, 10/16/96)

U.S. Army Attacked (NYT, 7/5/97)

Sensitivity Training — Army Style (WSJ, 1/19/98)

Helpful Hints (e-mails, 10/30/01)

Suggested Readings

These are a few of the books that have influenced what I pass off as thinking or that touch on the theme of Newspeak in some obscure fashion. I guarantee that I've actually read at least three pages of each book and that you can probably learn much more from their pages than from my ramblings.

Adorno, Theodor W. *Minima Moralia: Reflections from Damaged Life*. Trans. E.F.N. Jephcott. London: Verso, 1974.

Alinsky, Saul. *Rules for Radicals: A Practical Primer for Realistic Radicals*. New york: Vintage Books, 1989.

Bagddikan, Ben H. *The Media Monopoly*. Boston: Beacon Press, 1997.

Bellah, Robert, et al. *Habits of the Heart: Individualism and Commitment in American Life*. Berkeley: University of California Press, 1985.

Bruno, Kenny and Jed Greer. *Greenwash: The Reality Behind Corporate Environmentalism*. New York: Apex Press, 1996.

Chomsky, Noam and Edward Herman. *Manufacturing Consent: The Political Economy of the Mass Media*. New York: Pantheon Books, 1988.

De Graaf, John, David Wann and Thomas H. Naylor. *Affluenza: The All-Consuming Epidemic*. San Francisco: Berrett-Koehler, 2001.

Glendinning, Chellis. *My Name is Chellis and I'm in Recovery From Western Civilization*. Boston: Shambhala Publications, 1994.

Ehrenreich, Barbara. *Fear of Falling: The Inner Life of the Middle Class*. New York: Harper Collins, 1990.

Ewen, Stuart. *PR! : A Social History of Spin*. New York: Basic Books, 1996.

Faludi, Susan. *Backlash: The Undeclared War Against American Women*. New York: Crown Publishers, 1991.

Fromm, Erich. *Escape From Freedom*. New York: Holt, Rhinehart & Winston, 1941.

Gatto, John. *Dumbing Us Down: The Hidden Curriculum of Compulsory Schooling*. Gabriola Island: New Society Publishers, 1991.

Greider, William. *Who Will Tell the People: The Betrayal of American Democracy*. New York: Simon & Schuster, 1992.

Hardt, Michael and Antonio Negri. *Empire*. Cambridge: Harvard University Press, 2000.

Hightower, Jim. *There's Nothing in the Middle of the Road but Yellow Stripes and Dead Armadillos*. New York: Harper Collins, 1998.

Howard, Philip. *The Death of Common Sense: How Law is Suffocating America*. New York: Warner Books, 1994.

Huxley, Aldous. *Brave New World*. New York: Harper Perennial, 1998.

Ivins, Molly. *You've Got to Dance With Them What Brung You: Politics in the Clinton Years*. New York: Random House, 1999.

Jensen, Carl and Project Censored. *20 Years of Censored News*. New York: Seven Stories Press, 1997.

Klein, Naomi. *No Logo: Taking Aim at the Brand Bullies*. New York: Picador, 2000.

Lasch, Christopher. *The Culture of Narcissism: American Life in an Age of Diminishing Expectations*. New York: W. W. Norton & Co., 1979.

Lasn, Kalle. *Culture Jam: The Uncooling of America*. New York: Eagle Brook, 2000.

Lee, Martin A. and Norman Solomon. *Unreliable Sources: A Guide to Detecting Bias in the News Media*. New York: Carol Publishing, 1990.

Loeb, Paul. *Soul of a Citizen: Living With Conviction in a Cynical Time*. New York: St. Martin's Press, 1999.

David Loy, *A Buddhist History of the West: A Study of Lack*. Albany: State University of New York Press, 2002.

Lutz, William. *The New Doublespeak: Why No One Knows What Anyone's Saying Anymore*. New York: Harper Collins, 1996.

Macy, Joanna R. and Molly Young Brown. *Coming Back to Life: Practices to Reconnect Our Lives, Our World*. Gabriola Island: New Society Publishers, 1998.

MacIntyre, Alaisdaire. *Beyond Virtue: A Study in Moral Theory*. Notre Dame: University of Notre Dame Press, 1981.

Marcuse, Herbert. *One-Dimensional Man: Studies in the Ideology of Advanced Industrial Society*. Boston: Beacon Press, 1964.

McChesney, Robert. *Rich Media, Poor Democracy: Communication Politics in Dubious Times*. Urbana: University of Illinois Press, 2000.

Moore, Michael. *Downsize This: Random Threats from an Unarmed American*. New York: Crown Publishers, 1996.

Orwell, George. *1984*. New York: New American Library, 1990.

Putnam, Robert D. *Bowling Alone: The Collapse and Revival of American Community*. New York: Simon & Schuster, 2000.

Postman, Neil. *Amusing Ourselves to Death: Public Discourse in the Age of Show Business*. New York: Penguin Books, 1986.

Roszak, Theodore, Mary E. Gomes and Allen Kanner, eds. *Ecopsychology: Restoring the Earth, Healing the Mind*. San Francisco: Sierra Club Books, 1995.

Schiller, Herbert. *Culture Inc.: The Corporate Takeover of Public Expression*. New York: Oxford University Press, 1989.

Seed, John, Joanna Macy, Pat Fleming and Arne Naess, *Thinking Like a Mountain: Towards a Council of All Beings*. Gabriola Island: New Society Publishers, 1988.

Shephard, Paul. *Nature and Madness*. San Francisco: Sierra Club Books, 1982.

Shibayama, Zenkei. *The Gateless Barrier: Zen Comments on the Mumonkan.* Boston: Shambala, 2000.

Snyder, Gary. *The Practice of the Wild.* San Francisco: North Point Press, 1990.

Stauber, John and Sheldon Rampton. *Toxic Sludge is Good for You: Lies, Damn Lies and the Public Relations Industry.* Monroe: Common Courage Press, 1995.

Stone, I. F. *In a Time of Torment.* New York: Vintage Books, 1968.

Welton, Neva and Linda Wolf. *Global Uprising: Confronting the Tyrannies of the Twenty-First Century.* Gabriola Island: New Society Publishers, 2001.

Williams, Willam Appleman. *Empire as a Way of Life.* New York: Oxford University Press, 1980.

About the Author

Wayne Grytting grew up in the Lutheran ghetto of Seattle known as Ballard. Then came the Sixties, which he apparently did in style. After being tossed out of Reed College (where protesting was not recognized as a field of study), he earned a degree in philosophy from the University of Washington. This prepared him for his big career move, becoming a commercial halibut and salmon fish-

erman in Alaska. Maybe not the smartest move, as he decided twenty years later while trying to pull in a 200-pound halibut with a gaffhook onto the deck of a 58-foot boat in gale winds and 20-foot seas. With the thanks of the Coast Guard, he switched to teaching Special Education students (and facing emotional gale winds).

Wayne's first smart move was having a precocious daughter named Karena who was considerate enough to raise herself. Following a run for the state legislature as Washington's first and last Citizen's Party candidate, he began writing humorous op-eds for the Seattle Times, the Seattle P-I and the Seattle Weekly. In 1996 he turned to collecting examples of Orwellian Newspeak, aided by hundreds of "informers." His column was picked up by Z Magazine and spread over the Internet and the radio airwaves, and syndicated nationally to alternative news weeklies.

Wayne is married now to Kevin Castle, one of the first women to work on the docks of Seattle as a longshore-person. He relaxes by bicycling, kayaking, climbing mountains, writing incredibly bad poetry and attending weeklong Zen Buddhist meditation retreats. Wayne is available for speaking engagements and humor work-shops near sunny beaches. He can be contacted by e-mail at: wgrytt@scn.org or through his website: www.americannewspeak.org.

If you have enjoyed *American Newspeak*, you might also enjoy other

BOOKS TO BUILD A NEW SOCIETY

Our books provide positive solutions for people who want to
make a difference. We specialize in:

**Progressive Leadership • Resistance and Community
Environment and Justice • Conscientious Commerce
Natural Building & Appropriate Technology • New Forestry
Educational and Parenting Resources • Nonviolence
Sustainable Living • Ecological Design and Planning**

New Society Publishers

ENVIRONMENTAL BENEFITS STATEMENT

New Society Publishers has chosen to produce this book on recycled paper made
with **100% post consumer waste**, processed chlorine free, and old growth free.

For every 5,000 books printed, New Society saves the following resources:[1]

29	Trees
2,609	Pounds of Solid Waste
2,870	Gallons of Water
3,744	Kilowatt Hours of Electricity
4,742	Pounds of Greenhouse Gases
20	Pounds of HAPs, VOCs, and AOX Combined
7	Cubic Yards of Landfill Space

[1]Environmental benefits are calculated based on research done by the Environmental Defense Fund and
other members of the Paper Task Force who study the environmental impacts of the paper industry.

For a full list of NSP's titles, please call **1-800-567-6772** *or check out our web site at:*

www.newsociety.com

NEW SOCIETY PUBLISHERS